Praise for

FEARLESS IN 21 DAYS

"From the moment we began our interview with Sarah Ball on *Lifeline Today*, we knew that her story was one that had to be told. FEARLESS IN 21 DAYS is an instructional and faith-filled guide to overcoming crippling anxiety. As pastors and television ministers, we will be placing this into the hands of as many anxiety sufferers as we can. For ministry leaders, this book is an invaluable tool to better equip you to counsel others. Sarah's vulnerable story of her personal journey out of anxiety, OCD, and depression, along with practical tools, spiritual truths, and unwavering faith, makes this book beyond inspiring."

—Dick and Joan Deweert, pastors of Third Day Church,
founders of Dominion Media, and
cohosts of *Lifeline Today*

"FEARLESS IN 21 DAYS by Sarah Ball presents a refreshing blend of humor, practical insight, and biblical perspective on how to break free from anxiety. This book offers readers practical steps based in solid science, biblical truth, and honest authenticity that bring hope for real change. As someone who has struggled with anxiety, I'm delighted to endorse this book."

—Shelly Beach, author, speaker, consultant, and
winner of the Christy, Selah, Reader's Favorite,
and Golden Scroll Awards

"FEARLESS IN 21 DAYS is your breakthrough in a book. Whatever your story, Sarah will show you that you can live a fearless and joyful life. She thought she would never survive anxiety and depression, yet she did, and she's living proof that you can overcome, too. The wisdom of Sarah's whole life approach shows that healing an anxiety disorder is not just a physical problem fixed by medication, nor a spiritual problem healed by prayer, nor a mental issue prevented by therapy. It is all of the above. Following Sarah's insights will give you a prognosis for wellness."

—Bob Jones, lead pastor of North Pointe Church,
Edmonton, Alberta

"Sarah Ball's personal stories are relatable to women drowning in their own anxiety and depression, yet she throws them a lifeline of hope and light. Her candor and humor are also refreshing in a society where so many feel they need to hide behind a curtain of shame. Many thanks to Sarah for writing a book that will no doubt help thousands, if not millions, of women overcome their deepest pain . . . and then encourage them to be fearless!"

—Elizabeth Oates, author of *Mending Broken Branches*,
cofounder of Project Restoration Ministry

"In FEARLESS IN 21 DAYS, Sarah Ball offers lots of practical advice to her fellow Christians burdened by anxiety, panic attacks, and obsessive thinking. She comes alongside readers with symptoms similar to hers and offers a large measure of encouragement and hope. Her book is a great resource to believers suffering from anxiety."

—Stephen Grcevich, MD, president and founder of Key
Ministry, author of *Mental Health and the Church*

"It's pretty easy to be fear-filled in today's tumultuous world, but whether your anxiety is overtaking you or is just a subtle theme in the background of your mind, Sarah Ball's own epic battle with depression and anxiety brings incredible hope to all of us. Your reality today does not have to be your forever and Sarah shows us step-by-step how to walk out of full-blown anxiety into a life of peace and hope. This is a must-read!"

—Cheryl Weber, cohost and
senior executive producer of *100 Huntley Street*

"FEARLESS IN 21 DAYS is the remarkable story of one woman's victory over her anxiety disorder. But it is much more than that. It's a resource and guide to help conquer the fear that's at the heart of this disorder. It uses biblical truth to clear up many of the misconceptions that swirl around this mental illness, and yet it emphasizes the importance of well-rounded therapies that address a person's physical, mental, emotional, and spiritual needs. Best of all, it provides a day-by-day plan that puts readers on the road to recovery, too."

—Jolene Philo, author of *Does My Child Have PTSD?
What to Do When Your Child Is Hurting from the Inside Out*

FEARLESS

in 21 days

A SURVIVOR'S GUIDE
TO OVERCOMING ANXIETY

SARAH E. BALL

FaithWords

New York   Nashville

Copyright © 2018 by Sarah E. Ball

Cover design by Faceout Studio, Tim Green. Cover photograph by Stocksy, Jordi Rulló. Cover copyright © 2018 by Hachette Book Group, Inc.

FaithWords
Hachette Book Group
1290 Avenue of the Americas, New York, NY 10104
faithwords.com
twitter.com/faithwords

First Edition: January 2018

FaithWords is a division of Hachette Book Group, Inc. The FaithWords name and logo are trademarks of Hachette Book Group, Inc.

The publisher is not responsible for websites (or their content) that are not owned by the publisher.

The Hachette Speakers Bureau provides a wide range of authors for speaking events. To find out more, go to www.hachettespeakersbureau.com or call (866) 376-6591.

Scriptures noted (NKJV) are taken from the New King James Version®. Copyright © 1982 by Thomas Nelson. Used by permission. All rights reserved.

Scriptures noted (ISV) are taken from The Holy Bible: International Standard Version. Release 2.0, Build 2015.02.09. Copyright © 1995–2014 by ISV Foundation. ALL RIGHTS RESERVED INTERNATIONALLY. Used by permission of Davidson Press, LLC.

Scriptures noted (NIV) are taken from the Holy Bible, New International Version®, NIV®. Copyright © 1973, 1978, 1984, 2011 by Biblica, Inc.™ Used by permission of Zondervan. All rights reserved worldwide. www.zondervan.com. The "NIV" and "New International Version" are trademarks registered in the United States Patent and Trademark Office by Biblica, Inc.™

Scriptures noted (NLT) are taken from the Holy Bible, New Living Translation, copyright © 1996, 2004, 2007 by Tyndale House Foundation. Used by permission of Tyndale House Publishers, Inc., Carol Stream, Illinois 60188. All rights reserved.

Scriptures noted (NASB) are taken from the NEW AMERICAN STANDARD BIBLE®, Copyright © 1960, 1962, 1963, 1968, 1971, 1972, 1973, 1975, 1977, 1995 by The Lockman Foundation. Used by permission.

Scriptures noted (ESV) are from The ESV® Bible (The Holy Bible, English Standard Version®). ESV® Permanent Text Edition® (2016). Copyright © 2001 by Crossway, a publishing ministry of Good News Publishers. The ESV® text has been reproduced in cooperation with and by permission of Good News Publishers. Unauthorized reproduction of this publication is prohibited. All rights reserved.

Scriptures noted (RSV) are from the Revised Standard Version of the Bible, copyright © 1946, 1952, and 1971 the Division of Christian Education of the National Council of the Churches of Christ in the United States of America. Used by permission. All rights reserved.

Scriptures noted (MSG) are taken from The Message. Copyright © 1993, 1994, 1995, 1996, 2000, 2001, 2002. Used by permission of NavPress Publishing Group.

Library of Congress Control Number: 2017951513

ISBNs: 978-1-4789-2289-6 (hardcover); 978-1-4789-2287-2 (ebook)

Printed in the United States of America

LSC-C

10 9 8 7 6 5 4 3 2 1

To Kevin Ball
for your fearless love

To Adora, Chandler, Klara, Shepard, and Spencer
for giving me purpose in the valley

Contents

Contents

Contents

Contents

FEARLESS
IN 21 DAYS

Panic to Praise

❦

I paced my home trying to think of the best place to lie down in case I died. My heart was pounding, and I felt an immense amount of chest pressure and pain. I was light-headed, weak, and couldn't catch my breath. It wasn't a great day to die, really, because I had my five kids at home plus two more kids sleeping over. How would I explain this to their parents? My husband was at work, and everyone in the house was asleep. My red sofa seemed like the most appropriate place to perish, so I slowly unlocked the front door, made my way over to the couch, curled up into a ball in my favorite morning coffee groove, and then dialed 911.

The kids slept through the whole ordeal as the paramedics knocked on the door and excused their way into the house. They found me right away, since a pale, shaking, hyperventilating woman on a red couch is a fairly easy thing to spot. They calmly assessed me and asked if it was okay to sit on my IKEA coffee table. "Have you been under a lot of stress lately?" one asked. "We can take you to the hospital to make sure, but we are confident that this is a panic attack and you are not in any danger."

My dramatic near-death experience was a panic attack.

I was instructed to get some rest and was told I would feel better in the morning. The ambulance pulled away, and I crawled back into bed—humiliated, terrified, still trembling, and completely unaware of the journey that lay ahead. I was stepping into the darkest season of my life, and this was just the prelude.

That one day of panic turned into a full-blown panic disorder, causing me several panic attacks a day, continuing for months. I couldn't shower, I couldn't drive my kids to school, I couldn't eat, and some days I couldn't even leave my bed. My body trembled relentlessly, I constantly felt like my throat was closing in, my chest was heavy and tight, and my heart raced uncontrollably, even as I slept. The worst part was the horrifying sensation of impending doom and death. Fears dominated my thoughts, and thoughts ignited my fears. There were no specific triggers (unless you call a wind gust a trigger, or a doorbell). I feared going crazy. I lost total control over my body and mind, and I felt drained of all stability. I was afraid for my life, and I was afraid *of* my life.

When I realized that this was not going away on its own, I entered counseling. I was desperate and ready for God to take me through whatever healing I needed (or so I thought). I wanted to get it over with as fast as possible, because I wanted out as fast as possible.

My first appointment with the counselor was an hour long. The last thirty minutes were spent debriefing why I was there, but the first thirty minutes were spent talking me down from a panic attack, right there in the office. How humiliating. But even with months of counseling and prayer, I was still battling panic attacks and anxiety daily. As months passed with no progress, I began to grow weary of the day-to-day anxiety battle, and soon that battle began to manifest as depression and despair. Like Scripture says, "Anxiety in the heart of man causes depression" (Proverbs 12:25 NKJV).

This was not supposed to happen to a strong woman like me. I was a ministry leader at church and a mom of five children who once lived happily on a diet of stress and chaos and browsed Pinterest for inspirational meals. People looked up to me. I was the writer who encouraged people to stay strong in their faith. I was the friend who counseled and comforted. I was the life of the party, always making others laugh. I was superblogger, oldest child, and devoted wife. These breakdowns weren't supposed to happen to a woman like me; they happened to broken people and to people who didn't know the Lord. "Pride precedes destruction; an arrogant spirit appears before a fall" (Proverbs 16:18 ISV).

At the urging of my pastor, my husband, and my friends, I went to see my family doctor. I tried to convince him that I could get through this without medication, that I wasn't *that* bad. And then after I finished trying to convince him I was doing better, I had to pause our conversation for another panic attack in his office. Score: two for two. My husband squeezed my left hand as my doctor, who was also a Christian, held my right hand. "Even Jesus got weary," he comforted, and I sobbed. I was desperate for relief yet ashamed at the same time. I could not handle another moment, another attack, or another thought.

My decline was now exposed. No more have-it-all-together,

no more supermom, no more "How do you do it all?" Agoraphobia, the fear of leaving my home or being around a lot of people, was crowding in. I had lost fifteen pounds; I couldn't take care of my family anymore; I trembled when I talked; I avoided people and declined invitations. Then it got worse.

I started noticing myself hiding medications that were lying around. I wasn't hiding them from my children; I was hiding them from myself. I had this intense fear that if I got hit with despair I might take them all, or maybe I would lose my mind during a panic attack and try to end my life.

But it didn't stop there. I became so afraid of potentially harmful objects that I once grabbed a stool and put the bottle of bleach on the highest shelf in the laundry room, out of my reach, so that *I* wouldn't drink it. I started avoiding using knives, plastic bags, and ropes—anything that could ever be used to harm myself or someone else. I double-checked and triple-checked harmful objects. I needed to ensure that these items were safely stored away. From *me*.

I was developing symptoms of obsessive-compulsive disorder (OCD), or, to be more precise, harm OCD. I was bombarded by an irrational fear that I would lose control and hurt myself or, worse, someone else. The repetitive habits and checking that we commonly associate with OCD were growing in me, just to ease the thoughts and dissipate the anxiety.

Now, we all get bizarre imaginative thoughts from time to time, such as wondering if anyone would miss us if we drove off a bridge. We dismiss them as bizarre and then go on with the day. But a thought like that to people suffering from OCD can have them in the fetal position, avoiding bridges altogether or creating a ritual to ease the fear when they cross over one. I thought OCD happened to other women who were more uptight than I was and obsessed over cleanliness.

And then it happened to me.

Then what? you're probably wondering.

I pulled into the garage after an exhausting evening out with my children. I sat in my messy minivan and stared vacantly at my hands as they gripped the steering wheel. I began wringing the wheel back and forth like a dishrag. A new intense thought was flooding my mind, a thought I had never had before: *I'm just so tired; let's just not do this anymore.* I heard the sound of the garage door close behind me, and even though I had been trying to fight off harmful thoughts for quite some time, this was the first moment suicide became an option. I quickly unloaded the kids and ran into the house. I deeply understood in that moment that I was not just fighting for peace of mind anymore; I was fighting for my life.

I was clammy and panicked. I did not want to be alone, but I also unquestionably did not want to share these thoughts with anyone else.

Concerned by my frantic behavior, my husband asked, "Are you okay?"

"I'm fine," I lied as I handed off the kids for bedtime. I hurried to my bedroom. *How does God deal with suicide? Would I really go to hell? How would my family deal with it? Would I ever actually have the guts to do it?* I locked my door, longing to leave these forceful thoughts on the other side of it, but they followed me to my bed, the place I always ran to when I was afraid, the place I had been spending most of my days. I grabbed my Bible and flung it open. I was desperate for God to jump out and just hold me and promise me everything was going to be okay. I didn't want to read it. I just wanted it to work.

This was when I had a standoff with God and my Bible. "I either trust You, God, or I succumb. Your Word is either true, or I lose everything." What choice did I have at that moment? What else is there when the thought of death is comforting? I couldn't talk myself out of terror anymore; God had to. I couldn't reason with the suicidal thoughts; the Scriptures had to. It was my last resort.

As I began to read, speak, and pray God's Word, I felt like a child dressed in oversize armor, tripping over her own feet with no strength to lift a sword. I didn't know how to make the Bible verses I read work—how to "take my thoughts captive," how to let "perfect love cast out fear," or how to "meditate on His Word day and night." All I sort of knew was that this Bible—the one I had spent the last fifteen years of my life reading figuratively—could renew my mind. It was then that I made the decision to take each word that God breathed *literally*.

Healing is a process, especially healing complex conditions like anxiety and depression. When it comes to restoring the mind, a miraculous healing would bring relief like gulping in air after being held underwater for longer than we can handle, and I believe it's possible. However, if we do not take the time to labor through the tearing down of false mind-sets, lies, habits, and other sources of our anxiety, we will always risk returning to captivity. To be truly set free is to walk it out with God, even if it seems like the long way out.

God led me on a journey of healing with the guidance of His Word. What I was surprised to learn through that process was that God needed my body whole, my mind whole, and my spirit whole. Why? Because He loves *all* of me!

I now live free from crippling anxiety, panic disorder, suicidal depression, and OCD. God was faithful to renew my mind, restore my hope, and grant me the peace I desperately prayed for. A single day has not gone by where I have not thought about all that God has brought me out of. I praise the Lord that He was the One who brought me from panic to praise, and I know in my heart that His desire is to bring you there, too. I hope that my story and this book will help you to reclaim your life, find that lost hope again, and begin to live your days in joy and fearlessness.

I know you probably aren't completely convinced, because you are weary. Weary of waking up trembling, if you slept at all. Weary of your life revolving around your anxiety. Weary of fighting off panic attacks daily. Weary of praying the same prayers for peace; weary of the torment, the thoughts, the physical sensations, and the mental anguish.

You are not sure how you got to this point. Am I right? Chances are you were once a very strong, independent, busy, capable person whom many people depended on, but now you hide in bathroom stalls to talk yourself down from panic attacks. Maybe your story is that you have dealt with this from childhood or adolescence, and you have finally reached a point where you want freedom. Or maybe you have decided that this is just who you are, and now you are looking for a book to help you cope better. Your desire for living a joyful, fearless life has faded.

You have tried everything, haven't you? You have prayed one thousand prayers and you have read every book on anxiety, yet you are still panicked, still avoiding crowds, still depressed, and still white-knuckled when you have to drive.

Whatever your story, however you got here, I am here to tell you that you *can* live a fearless and joyful life. I didn't think I would ever survive it, either. Yet I did, and I am living proof that you can overcome anxiety, too.

When I was in the depths of my mental breakdown, I could not find the right words to describe what it felt like to be subjected to daily anxiety and panic attacks. Then one day, I stumbled upon a different translation of 1 John 4:18: "There is no fear in love; but perfect love casts out fear, because fear involves torment" (NKJV). Tears poured down my cheeks, because I had finally found a word to describe what was happening to my mind: torment.

Tormented daily for months, I could not sleep, eat, or function. Showering was terrifying, the phone ringing would send me into a panic, and running my household of seven became an impossible task. I was once a very strong, capable, and busy woman, and then I became a mental health statistic. According to the Anxiety Disorders Association of Canada[1] and the Anxiety and Depression Association of America,[2] 12 percent of Canadians and 18 percent of Americans will have at least one episode of anxiety disorder in their lifetimes. Welcome to the club.

When I began writing and speaking out about my illness, I

began to hear from others who were tormented by the same illness—people you would never suspect, living in anguish, just like me and just like you. I realized very quickly that I was not alone, and that 12 to 18 percent is a very big number. I began to recognize the signs of people who were living with chronic anxiety—like the guy who paced the back of the church on Sunday mornings, the lady who rambled a mile a minute at dinner parties, or the man who never left his house. I began to see and recognize the plague of anxiety, the people it affected, the complexity of it all. I became sadly aware that anxiety can ravage anyone—all races, all ages, all religions, and all sexes. Anxiety doesn't care who you are; it torments whomever it wants.

Fear chose me, and I was completely overcome and desperate to find a way out. There are hundreds of conflicting techniques, programs, and advice for treating anxiety, but most of the information I found was about *coping* with anxiety, not eliminating it. There was no way I was going to have this noose around my neck for the rest of my life. So I kept digging, researching, talking, asking, and reading. Most of all I kept seeking God for a breakthrough. A good Father listens to His kids, and God began showing me the way out.

Like a woman on a mission, I searched everywhere for answers and solutions. I went through therapy, read books, begged God, followed programs, listened to sermons, begged God, visited my doctor, begged God some more, and wore out my Google page. I was so desperate for deliverance that I would do anything to be set free. I began to sift through all the information I could find on curing anxiety and panic. There was a lot of nonsense, but there were a lot of treasures, too. Through this God-led journey, I learned a lot about our minds, our emotions, our spirits, and our physical bodies, and I slowly began to discover truths that were key to my freedom.

I soon understood that truly healing an anxiety disorder was not just addressing a physical problem that could be fixed by medication, nor a spiritual problem healed by prayer, nor a mental issue prevented by therapy. It was not any one of the above, but rather *all* of the above. Each part of our beings is interconnected, completely dependent on one another, and affected by our actions. When I began to take all aspects of myself seriously, nurturing it all, I began to see the greatest breakthrough in healing I'd ever had.

So many times when we seek freedom in certain areas of our lives, we search for one tool to repair our brokenness. Often people suffering from anxiety will opt for only medication, or try naturopathic treatment, or seek healing only through prayer. But the secret to overcoming a disorder like anxiety is treating the whole person. We must begin to understand that there is a powerful connection between our thoughts, our physical habits, and our relationship with God. Without a healing attention to all three—body, mind, and spirit—we will never fully recover, because God created us as one.

When I fully grasped this truth, that healing must take place throughout my whole self, I began to focus on whole healing—all facets of my being: my body, my mind, and my spirit. I soon began to experience total healing through the miraculous power of prayer, the nourishing support of nutrition and exercise, and the empowerment of taking my thoughts captive.

That discovery led me to a path of freedom, and that freedom has led me to you.

I grieved deeply at the idea of another person being tortured by their mind, day and night, like I was. I knew that when God pulled me out of this dark pit, I would reach my hand back and pull others out. My compassion made me determined to help others like you.

Many of my blog readers and Facebook followers followed me through my breakdown season. I never intended to write much about my anxiety, and I for sure didn't want to talk about my OCD or depression. I kept it hidden for a long time. I didn't know what to say, because I didn't know what was happening to me, and I didn't know how to get out. As I began to catch my breath, God began nudging me to share. He kept calling me to vulnerability and challenging me that my story, this testimony, was not mine to keep. He had a purpose through all of this, and I chose to answer the call.

Then I heard a loud voice in heaven say:

> Now have come the salvation and the power
>> and the kingdom of our God,
>> and the authority of his Messiah
> For the accuser of our brothers and sisters,
>> who accuses them before our God day and night,
>> has been hurled down.
> They triumphed over him
>> by the blood of the Lamb
>> and by the word of their testimony.

REVELATION 12:10–11 NIV

I labored and wrestled with vulnerability. What would I share? What would I reveal? I forced myself to sit down and write as honestly as I could. I opened up about my journey through the anxiety, the depression, the OCD, the despair, the strain on my family and my friends, and my anger at God. I held nothing back. Some days I cried, feeling exposed to the world. Some days I wrestled to hit Publish. Then, slowly, my posts of deep suffering and vulnerability became posts of victories, celebrations, revelations, and joy, and ultimately out of that came *Fearless in 21 Days*.

I created the "Fearless in 21 Days" series on my blog to give people hope, to lead them to God's healing power, and to pass on practical wisdom. I just wanted to help people in a tangible way—spiritually, physically, and mentally. What I didn't expect when blogging the series was the response from readers, the shares, and the referrals from anxiety sites, nurses, friends, and other blogs.

These responses taught me one thing: Anxiety sufferers don't want another self-help book on breathing techniques. Trust me, I know. They want to be heard and understood by someone who has lived through it firsthand. Someone who can relate to the feeling of disassociation or the fear of going crazy. Someone who can empathize with the irrational but intense fear of bridges, bleach, and sickness. Someone who can describe the absolute terror a thought can bring on or how humiliating it is to be seen trembling in social situations. Sufferers want real knowledge, real hope, and real answers, but most of all they want compassion. Don't you?

I am not a therapist, I am not a doctor, and I make no claims to being a medical professional, but I am you, healed. I am you, better. I am you, whole. I am you, fearless! I know how one simple thought can ravage your body, putting you into shock, or how fast you can lose the ability to be around people due to the fear of having another panic attack. I am an expert at splashing cold water on my face just to snap out of the anxiety fog and clear my head, and I am an expert at not being able to get out of bed to fulfill my greatest mission as a mother. I still have the get-well cards my children wrote me as I lay in bed, wasting away and trembling for months on end.

May I ask you this? How many people have told you that you will get through this, and you just want to punch them? Sorry to tell you (as I duck), but it is true. You *will* get through this, and I believe God has called me to show you how.

How to Use This Book

This is not a breeze-through book, and you do not have to let your drive and perfectionism tell you that you have to complete it in twenty-one days. Read it at your own pace, prayerfully, and with commitment. It is up to God to show you the way you should go, but it is up to you to walk yourself there.

Before you begin, I encourage you to have a conversation with your doctor. It is important to ensure that what you are dealing with is indeed an anxiety issue and not an underlying health issue. Also, a thorough checkup can help ease any underlying health fears. This book is *not* meant to replace medication, therapy, or your spiritual support; everything is to be discerned by you and those who are responsible for your spiritual, mental, and physical care.

Journaling is an important part of working through this book. Journaling helps us to see our progress and go back over what we have learned. You will need your Bible for reference, and you will need people who can pray with you through some of the things I will be showing you, especially when we cover spiritual deliverance and healing the past. Most of all, you will need to hold on to the hope and joy that freedom *is* possible!

Creation of Fear

❧

Fear makes us feel our humanity.

—Benjamin Disraeli, *Vivian Grey*

God created all things for good. He created the heavens and saw that it was good. He created the animals and saw that it was good. He created fear and saw that it was good. Satan, on the other hand, is *not* a creator; he created nothing with his own power and might. Satan has always taken what was meant for good and breathed deception into it. He has done the same with love, with families, with religion, with health; and he has done it with fear. Today, we are going to expose Satan's twisted version of fear and look into God's original design and purpose for this fear and trembling.

Fear Is Our Greatest Guardian

Healthy fear keeps us from doing stupid things like falling off cliffs and jumping into zoo compounds full of hungry lions. Fear keeps us from dangerous situations and keeps all our limbs intact. Without fear, we would all be very brave, but also very dead.

I am Canadian. I am well aware that the live versions of those cute little stuffed bears we cuddle with at night could actually rip us apart in seconds. When we as a family travel to the Rocky Mountains and see a bear, elk, moose, or, worse, a mountain lion, we pause, resist the urge to pee our pants, and back away slowly. The inexperienced tourists, on the other hand, are often blissfully fearless. This lack of fear leads many tourists to a potentially deadly encounter as they try to get a closer look or take a better picture. But it takes only one growl or charging elk to kick-start a tourist's fear response.

I laugh every time I think of the day my friend and I took our children on a mountain hike in Waterton National Park. I had four of my children with me, ages six to fourteen, and she had her two boys. We had just reached the entrance to this two-hour trail with our backpacks full of snacks, bug spray, sunscreen, and water, when we heard screaming coming from the path ahead. "RUUUUUNNNN!" several voices yelled.

We froze, trying to understand what we were to run from, who was screaming, and where to run to. We had no idea if it was a grizzly bear or a swarm of bees. So we ran. All eight of us raced back to our vehicle and crouched behind it. We were out of breath and sweating. Soon we saw two sets of tourists bolt out of the forest, bellowing, "Run! Sheep!"

"Sheep?!" We laughed in relief. It turned out that these hikers had cornered a group of bighorn mountain sheep that were descending down the trail. The hikers wanted to take a picture of the mom and the supercute baby, but the daddy bighorn sheep was not having it. After the hikers escaped their close call of being literally butted out of the forest, they stood around flush-faced, panicked, and sharing with anyone who would listen about their life-and-death experience. The sheep, now on the main road, recovering from their own panic, stood and glared. We reassured the kids the trail was clear, took a far-off picture of the peeved sheep, and off we went, back onto the trail for a lovely hike.

Aren't we thankful that most of us are born with the common sense to protect ourselves from danger? God has given each of us a rational brain that guides us and protects us from potential threats like mama bears and hormonal bighorn mountain sheep. That guide is our fear and panic response.

Panic Keeps Us Alive

We can look at these poor hikers and continue to make fun of them or we can use this as a learning tool. What was happening to them in that moment was a potentially life-threatening situation, and we are going to continue to use this scenario to better understand fear. Their bodies, minds, and spirits, within a split second, collaborated and came up with the same ambition: "We want to survive this sheep stampede." With this in mind, their bodies were flung into full-on panic mode. In his book *Don't Panic: Taking Control of Anxiety Attacks*, R. Reid Wilson, PhD, describes what is happening in the mind and body during a panic attack. In this mode of panic, he explains, many things are happening all at once: Your heart is pounding, you have resorted to shallow breathing, your mind has begun racing and grasping for a plan, and you are possibly questioning your mortality.[1]

All three parts of these hikers' beings—bodies, minds, and spirits—were working in tandem to protect themselves and help them survive this potential bighorn sheep attack. Their hearts were pounding for a purpose: They were trying to flush blood to all the organs to create a wall of protection. Breathing feels shallow not because of a lack of oxygen, but because the body is actually taking in too much air, trying to fuel the brain into finding a way out. Thoughts are flooding the brain thanks to all the blood and oxygen that have just invaded, and the brain is trying to troubleshoot and act fast. In panic, our bodies and minds are preparing for impact. This is a good thing when trouble comes; it helps us to plan fast, to act fast, and to create the best possible chance of survival.

Wilson also describes the stages of a panic attack throughout our bodies. First, the mind receives a threat—the sheep. Second, the mind interprets the threat—those sheep horns are *huge*! Third, the mind decides how to react to the threat— sprint down the mountain and scream, "Ruuun! Sheep!" Last, it tells the body how to survive the threat—panic attack symptoms.[2]

It is important for us to understand how and why our bodies respond to panic, because understanding that a panic attack is the body's attempt to protect us eases the fear of the symptoms and sensations we experience. We will touch on this later, but when we are in a cycle of endless panic and anxiety, we begin to adopt a fear of *fear*. We become more afraid of having another panic attack than of the initial panic trigger. Understanding that fear was created by God for our protection will allow us to accept fear as God's design, versus resisting and running from it. It will also bring us closer to the original purpose of fear, which is worship.

Fear Is Created for Worship

Imagine being a firsthand witness to the creation of the earth— stars being told to shine, blue skies forming, waters filling all the crevices in the earth, and animals being molded by the commands of God. How would you react to this unfolding masterpiece?

Reflect on Noah and his family as they marveled at the downpour of rain falling from the sky unceasingly. They must have trembled as the earth slowly disappeared underneath the waves, waves that carried them far from their home and former way of life. They were firsthand witnesses to the great, manifested power of God.

Think of the shepherds, told of Jesus' birth by a procession of melodic angels filling the created sky:

An angel of the Lord appeared to them, and the glory of the Lord shone around them, and *they were terrified*. But the angel said to them, *"Do not be afraid. I bring you good news that will cause great joy for all the people. Today in the town of David a Savior has been born to you; he is the Messiah, the Lord. This will be a sign to you: You will find a baby wrapped in cloths and lying in a manger."*

Suddenly a great company of the heavenly host appeared with the angel, praising God and saying,

"Glory to God in the highest heaven,
and on earth peace to those on whom his favor rests."

LUKE 2:9–14 NIV (EMPHASIS MINE)

The shepherds were frozen in fear. Perhaps some of them ran or hid behind stones and trees. I personally would have grabbed a sheep or two to shield myself. Can you imagine their reaction to this angelic visit? We could feel sorry for the shepherds, being jolted and shaken, but let me ask you one question: What would it say about God if they had no intense emotional response to His glory? What if their response to this heavenly display was an unimpressed "Meh"? My prayer is that we never become numb to the presence of our God. It would say to me that He is lesser than or equal to us, and that is not at all the God we serve.

These shepherds reacted to their Abba Father's glory the way they were created to respond, in overwhelmed awe. They trembled, they sobbed, their palms were sweaty, their heads spun, and their minds raced as they tried to make sense of it all. Their bodies went weak and felt faint. Sound familiar? They were terrified!

What does this reaction say about God? Is He cruel? A tormentor? That is what Satan would have you believe, but the Bible says that God is love. And Paul, His beloved apostle, prayed that his readers would "*grasp* how wide and long and high and deep is *the love of Christ*, and to know this love that surpasses knowledge—that you may be filled to the measure of all the fullness of God" (Ephesians 3:18–19 NIV; emphasis mine). *God's* love is so exceedingly powerful, amazing, and beyond our comprehension that our human brains cannot fathom it— to the extent that we need prayer just to be able to grasp it!

If we have always equated fear with a negative emotion, then we have likely lived our lives avoiding fear at all cost. Are you taken aback when I say that fear is instead one of the greatest and most positive emotions there is? The purpose of fear is way more fundamental and glorious than just to save a limb or two—I believe that God created in us a physiological response of fear to worship Him.

True worship is a response to His glory, which is ultimately a display of His radiant love. We are so in awe of His splendor that we tremble. We are so taken aback by His majesty that we fall down. We are left so breathless by His beauty that we cannot speak: "Let all the earth fear the LORD; let all the inhabitants of the world stand in awe of Him" (Psalm 33:8 NKJV).

So why is anxiety crippling us into destruction if God has created fear as a response to His glory? I believe we have misplaced worship, that's why.

The fear you feel is not a curse or a faulty design. *It is misplaced worship.* Since the separation of humanity and God, the enemy of our soul overtook fear. Fear became blurred and distorted, just like all of the other pleasures God intended for good. Desire turned into lust, joy turned into sorrow, life turned into death, and worship turned into torment. The intense emotional responses to the overwhelming love and power of God have been replaced with an intense emotional response to the power and intimidation of Satan.

Here's an equation that may help you better understand:

FEAR ROOTED IN LOVE = THE EMOTION OF AWE
FEAR ROOTED IN LIES = THE EMOTION OF TORMENT

Satan's entire purpose for deceiving Adam and Eve was to gain their worship, to have them trust in his lies instead of God's truth. If Satan can keep us trembling at his lies, we turn our attention away from God and respond in awe to Satan's power. God is love, and His promises have always been to prosper us, to give us a future and a hope. Satan, through his threats and terrorizations, promises to harm us, not to prosper us; promises to kill us and destroy us, not to give us a future and a hope. We tremble in torment at his supposed power. We turn our worship toward the evil one. Yet the Word of God commands us, "Serve only the LORD your God and fear him alone" (Deuteronomy 13:4 NLT).

Fear—which was intended to allow our bodies and minds to feel fully alive, causing our spirits to leap within us and fall at His feet in awe—has turned into an emotion of torment: "There is no fear in love; but perfect love casts out fear, because fear involves torment. But he who fears has not been made perfect in love" (1 John 4:18 NKJV). Nevertheless, we are not victims; we are overcomers. And we can learn to silence the lies, push back the worldly fears, and turn our worship back to God.

My prayer with this book is that we succeed in taking back what Satan has stolen, push back against the temptation to misplace our worship, and renew our minds. The rest of this book, day by day, will bring you closer to this revelation and give you the tools needed to overcome. There are some lies we need to break off, some wounds we need to heal, and some truths we need to hear. The work has just begun, and I hope this understanding helps you to have a response of thankfulness to God for the emotion of fear rather than a response of hate. Fear is not our enemy; Satan is. Let's commit ourselves now to seeking God's love by opening our minds to the truth that He has come to set us free. And that starts now.

APPLICATION: When I began to understand the physiological science behind what was happening to my body and mind during a panic attack, it decreased my symptoms radically. Take time to study further the science behind God's perfect design. I recommend reading *Don't Panic* by R. Reid Wilson, PhD.[3] Why do you think understanding God's purpose for fear and the body's natural response to it might be helpful?

Day 2

Body-Mind Connection

❧

Pay mind to your own life, your own health, and wholeness. A bleeding heart is of no help to anyone if it bleeds to death.

—FREDERICK BUECHNER, *TELLING SECRETS*

Mental illnesses, such as anxiety disorders, are among the most misunderstood, misdiagnosed, and mistreated illnesses in the Christian faith. Sadly, many Christians who struggle with anxiety and panic are falsely led to believe that theirs is merely a spiritual struggle and they undergo humiliating attempts at deliverance. Some are also led to believe it's their fault because of sin or because their faith isn't enough to heal them. In reality, the majority of people I have talked to who struggle with severe anxiety have an incredibly dependent, vulnerable, and personal relationship with Jesus. Anxiety sufferers often resist lifesaving medication because other believers tell them it is sacrilegious, and they venture away from modern therapies because Christ should be enough. Yet Satan remains their biggest conversationalist, and they remain in complete terror and bondage, many tempted to despair. It is no wonder that Christians who suffer with anxiety and panic hide their illness in shame. Have you had to also?

When God created Adam, He made Adam in His image

(which was good). He created Adam with arms, legs, organs, and a mind. Our bodies were not an afterthought to our spirits. They were not created merely to house the Holy Spirit, but to work in unison with the Spirit of God. It is a beautifully crafted trinity, meant to flow in perfect harmony, meant to fulfill the greatest commandment of all—"Love the Lord your God with all *your heart* and with all *your soul* and with all *your* *strength* and with all *your mind*" (Luke 10:27 NIV; emphasis mine).

God's concern for our whole being was displayed by Jesus' compassion as He healed physical illnesses everywhere He went. Physical healing was, and still is, a sign of God's presence. He did not come merely to bring salvation, but to bring whole healing. "Now may the God of peace Himself sanctify you entirely; and may your *spirit* and *soul* and *body* be preserved complete, without blame at the coming of our Lord Jesus Christ" (1 Thessalonians 5:23 NASB; emphasis mine).

If you are serious about being free from anxiety, panic, and even depression, then you cannot deny your physical self. It must become an equal focus along with your mind and your spirit. God takes your health seriously, and so should you.

I was absolutely stunned by the physical expression of anxiety. My hair began falling out in handfuls, my muscles were weak, and I was clumsy and out of breath. I had dark circles under my eyes, and I had acne for the first time ever. My skin was dry and pale, and I began to lose weight rapidly. I had to stop looking at myself in the mirror daily because the lifeless stress on my face was hard to bear, and it only caused me more despair and anxiety.

I was convinced I was dying, and after thorough examinations and medical testing, my doctor was convinced it was all anxiety. I was a healthy thirty-six-year-old in a hundred-year-old anxious body, all thanks to my mind.

The good news is that God wants to restore not only your mental health, but also your physical health! Today I feel healthier and more energetic than I have in years. I am convinced it is because God has done a complete work in me. He has restored my strength, just like His Word promises.

I knew that if I wanted to become a person who was strong, healthy, mentally stable, and happy, then I would have to make my physical health a priority. Even now when I find myself slipping into old thought patterns, or depression starts to creep in, I flounder for a while, wondering why it has been a hard couple of days. Then I realize that my healthy lifestyle has slipped. No longer is my muffin top my motivation for putting down the salt-and-vinegar chips and going for a walk. My thoughts and emotions are.

The Physical Symptoms of Anxiety:

- Shortness of breath or hyperventilation
- Being easily fatigued
- Heart palpitations or a racing heart
- Chest pain or discomfort
- Trembling or shaking
- Choking feeling
- Feeling unreal or detached from your surroundings (depersonalization)
- Sweating

- Nausea or upset stomach
- Feeling dizzy, light-headed, or faint

- Muscle tension
- Numbness or tingling sensations
- Hot or cold flashes

(SOURCE: *DIAGNOSTIC AND STATISTICAL MANUAL OF MENTAL DISORDERS*, FIFTH EDITION)

Exercise

Walking became a lifeline for me. There were days my skin was literally crawling with anxiety, and the only way to burn off that negative energy was to walk it off. Other days I felt lifeless and zoned out. The only way through that fog was to walk, even though walking was the last desire I had on earth. According to Michael W. Otto, PhD, and Jasper A. J. Smits, PhD, those who exercise regularly are 25 percent less likely to develop depression or an anxiety disorder.[1] Exercise is one of the greatest preventive measures a person can take. I have heard many stories of people overcoming mental illnesses like depression with regular walks. The nice thing about walking is that you can use it as prayer time, too. "He gives strength to the weary and increases the power of the weak. Even youths grow tired and weary, and young men stumble and fall; but those who hope in the LORD will renew their strength. They will soar on wings like eagles; they will run and not grow weary, they will walk and not be faint" (Isaiah 40:29–31 NIV).

Start small! I was so extremely sick with anxiety that I could not leave my house. I remember the day I invited my friend over to "walk me." She held my arm. "You can do it," she said as she assisted my trembling body over the threshold of my front door. I had not left my house in days. I made it thirty feet and had to stop. I could not go any farther, physically or emotionally. I was beginning to fear leaving my house, and my body was frail from fear. My first intentional walk at my worst lasted five minutes before I begged to go back into the house. But I persisted daily, knowing it would help. It did help. It helped immensely. Soon those five minutes of walking turned into thirty, and now I jog for pleasure.

God designed our bodies to move, and move actively. Our racing minds require oxygen and blood flow to remain in full function. Our hearts—those fearful, palpitating hearts—need to be pushed and maxed. Our lungs—those shallow, uptight lungs—need a deep inhale. When we encourage our bodies to move, we, in turn, are telling our brains, "Everything is actually okay." Exercise increases endorphins, the "happy" hormones that you are deficient in right now, but did you know it also creates new brain cells? Exercise is absolutely essential in maintaining your overall health. That's why when God created Adam, He didn't say, "Now here's a pizza-and-pop tree and there's a comfy reclining bush." No, He told Adam to work! He provided Adam with fields to run in, trees to climb, mountains to conquer, oceans to swim in, and valleys to roll down. Creation was created for you to explore, and your body was created to explore it.

Exercise Tips

- If for some reason you can't walk, move your arms and do floor exercises, ANYTHING that gets you moving.

- Get your heart rate up for at least twenty minutes per day.

- Vary your exercise—sports, dancing, running—and make it fun!

- Exercise with someone. Social interaction *and* physical exercise is an anxiety-killing combo!

- Avoid strenuous exercise that may cause injury or burnout.

Nutrition

Nothing says mental chaos like sugar, caffeine, large amounts of alcohol, or unhealthy foods. Studies have shown that 80 percent of those struggling with emotional highs and lows recognized a connection between their mood and their food![2]

As a mom of five endlessly "starving" children, I am attuned to my children's moods and the connection to their nutrition. A day filled with hot dogs and birthday cake will usually end with a fit of tears. If my teen skips eating due to the coolness factor, I can expect an irrational outburst before dinner. My middle son is particularly sensitive. He might just begin to break down—tears, fears, and overreactions—but the cure is always food. As soon as he eats, it's like the emotional plane has landed.

Your anxious mind is overwhelmed, and your body is

exhausted trying to compensate for your endless thoughts. Healthy food is necessary for feeding your brain and creating a nutritional balance and calm. It will assist greatly in warding off your panic and anxiety.

Listen to your body. Did you have a rough day mentally? What did you eat that morning or the night before? Do you notice a connection between that glass of wine and your anxiety the next day? Begin to pay attention to what foods cause you grief and what foods actually help you. Your body wants to tell you!

Anxiety-Causing Food and Drink

Caffeine. I am back to drinking my lovely java now, thank goodness! However, during the peak of my anxiety I avoided it. The effects of caffeine can resemble the physical symptoms of anxiety, which could trigger an anxiety attack.

Sugar. Poor sugar; it's gotten such a bad reputation. Excess amounts of sugar are mind-killers. Your grandmother told you that, your first-grade health teacher told you that, the crazy wacko food documentaries tell you that. So why aren't you listening?! Excessive sugar is not good for your physical health, and it is not good for your mental health, either.

Alcohol. The sad truth is that about 25 percent of people with an anxiety and depression disorder struggle with substance abuse.[3] The even sadder truth is that the very thing that is being used to relieve anxiety and depression could actually be making it worse. Alcohol is a depressant and can be a devastating trap. I love my wine, but it didn't always love me. One glass at dinner was all I ever consumed at a time, but within an hour my anxious thoughts increased. During my breakdown, alcohol was something I had to avoid. Not only is it good to avoid for trigger reasons but also to reduce the risk of relying on drinking as a form of coping. If this is something you are struggling with, please seek professional help.

Hydration

Dehydration is more connected to anxiety than you may think. Keeping your body hydrated will keep your mind at ease and actually clear your muddled brain. If you feel faint and sluggish, chances are you just need a big drink of water. Dehydration can also cause heart palpitations, fatigue, and light-headedness, all those panic symptoms that spiral us into a panic attack. Your brain is 85 percent water, and if it is not hydrated, then it cannot work at its full potential. It is pretty simple, isn't it? Water won't cure anxiety, but it will greatly reduce those awful panicky symptoms and help the mind to heal and think more clearly.

Take Care of Your Whole Self

As much as I am advocating for you to listen to your body and begin to treat it with more care through nutrition and exercise, I want to remind you that in healing anxiety we must care for the whole person—body, mind, and spirit. Be careful not to blame all your anxiety on your physical health. I have met many people who have struggled with anxiety, and they go to great lengths to seek physical healing. People slather on essential oils, take herbal supplements or antidepressants, see many doctors, do crazy cleanses, and the list goes on and on. All of the above are suitable treatments in helping anxiety, but not in and of themselves.

Antianxiety/Antidepressant Prescription Medication

I have to be honest and tell you I was against antidepressants and antianxiety drugs until I trembled in my doctor's office begging for answers. I won't tell you yes, you should, or no, you should not. This is between you, your medical doctor, your therapist, and the Holy Spirit. Each case is unique, and medication can be a lifesaver for many. Medication does not heal your past or your way of thinking, and it does not reverse the weariness of your soul, but it can help in the physical realm of things and get you stable enough to deal with the root causes. In my opinion, medication should never be the end of your healing journey. It should be the beginning!

❧

APPLICATION: It's very difficult to add exercise to your life when you just want to stay curled up and hidden away, but it is so essential in easing anxiety. What small steps can you take today that are fun and easy to add to your lifestyle? What foods or drinks do you need to cut back on or eliminate from your diet?

Day 3

Stop the Panic

∽

Moses answered the people, "Do not be afraid. Stand firm and you will see the deliverance the LORD will bring you today. The Egyptians you see today you will never see again."

—EXODUS 14:13 NIV

Panic attacks are probably one of the most frightening experiences outside of an actual life-and-death situation. It is extremely hard to explain to people what a panic attack feels like if they have never experienced one. I have tried several times to explain, but the most common response is usually "Can't you just snap out of it?" Ha! I wish it were that simple!

Panic can hit at any time, anywhere, and a person suffering with a panic disorder is completely at the mercy of these unpredictable assaults. A panic attack is a recipe full of ingredients like extreme physical symptoms, distorted intense thoughts and sensations, and an unshakable sense of impending doom. There is no normal anymore for someone with this disorder. Try to function normally with a loaded gun pointed at your head, or try to carry on a conversation with someone as a bear approaches.

Out of the blue you begin to feel physical symptoms akin to what a heart attack would feel like. A pounding heart, a closed-up throat, the inability to take a deep breath, weakness, trembling, and you can fill in the rest, because there are too many disturbing symptoms to mention in one sentence. The fear that you are dying begins to heighten, and your mind becomes completely consumed with the panic you are feeling. Your body is thrown into massive physical anxiety, and mental anguish takes over.

It can be a daily battle for someone suffering with a panic disorder. Sometimes panic attacks can hit hourly. Sufferers can find themselves trying to function normally, never knowing when the next panic will overtake them. Panic doesn't stop there, though. It is rude and uninvited, and it can escalate into a disorder very quickly, which can lead to intensified anxiety and isolation. Some people who struggle with a panic disorder can become agoraphobic, afraid to leave their houses, afraid to drive, or afraid to be around people.

This was me. I went from being a socialite to being afraid to leave my bedroom. It was the only place I felt safe enough to cope in case a panic attack came on. The idea of having company, going to the grocery store, or attending a school function had me completely frozen. I was caught off guard by how isolated this disorder was making me. I was having panic attacks hourly, for months on end, even in my sleep or as I woke. Most of the attacks were completely unpredictable and uncontrollable. I would often just break down in tears before God, begging Him to deliver me. My biggest fear that triggered a panic attack was the fear of another panic attack, especially in a place that could cause me, or my family, great embarrassment. It was a nightmare, and my life was falling apart because of it—until one day I found the courage to face it head-on.

Facing Panic Head-On

The majority of people will at some point in their lives suffer from a single panic attack, but for today's purposes, we are talking about those of you who are having panic attacks on a regular basis. The main fuel that makes this terror burn is the fear of another attack. The fear of another horrible panic attack is actually keeping the panic alive. You become so afraid of these spontaneous assaults that it becomes the central theme of your fear.

My most embarrassing panic attack was at my very first therapy appointment. I was fighting one off in the waiting room, trying to hold it together. I had not left my house in days— except for a visit to my doctor (where I had one, too). I smiled as the therapist came out to greet me, and I managed to make small talk as he invited me to take a seat, but as soon as he asked, "What brings you here today?" I became so unglued by a panic attack that I could not even speak. My therapist calmly placed his notepad on the table and talked me down by encouraging me to breathe and relax. At that point, I don't think he needed much more introduction as to why I was there. I had a similar attack at my doctor's office, at church, at the grocery store, while driving, and too many others to recall. I know firsthand how these moments of terror can take over your life and how quickly they can drag you to despair, so I am going to get to the point.

How I Fought Panic Attacks and Won

I had stumbled through numerous resources on how to breathe and "picture a beach" to make my panic attacks go away. Nothing worked. Then I stumbled upon an audiobook by Dr. Claire Weekes, published in 1969,[1] back when panic disorders were called "nervous disorders," hence the term "nervous breakdown." She had developed a very successful treatment for overcoming panic, not by running from it but by facing it head-on. She taught me that the worst thing you can do during a panic attack is to run, fight, and become impatient, which is exactly how I had been treating my panic. Weekes went on to say that the only cure for panic attacks is to face each one, accept it, let it float past, and be patient as the panic flows through you. She stated that no matter how intense or how new the anxiety and panic symptoms become, you must continue to practice full acceptance. This was life-changing for me, and it taught me how to face this panic bully head-on. I won the battle with panic by telling it I wasn't afraid of it anymore. When it came to my panic, I thought of it as a school bully, a bully who was always threatening violence and flexing its muscles. This bully continued to dominate my thoughts, just like the bullies at school. They always seem to show up everywhere, and so we fear every corner, wondering when they will pop out. Then we avoid the cafeteria, the library, the hallways, and eventually check out of school altogether. This bully continued to torment me, until I stopped running away.

My poor brother was a victim of bullying when he was in

sixth grade. Day after day he would come home in tears, after hiding from the bullies who waited to pounce on him every day after school. One day he burst through the door in tears and in terror. "They're chasing me!" he cried out. Well, as an eighth grader and the bossy older sister, I threw on my neon high-tops and bolted up the alley. Sure enough, the bullies saw me coming, and I yelled, "Hey, you!" They turned around in surprise, frozen in confusion at this five-foot, ninety-pound brunette storming up the alley, shoelaces trailing behind. I grabbed the shorter one by his shirt and pushed him against the fence. "If you bug my brother one more time, I am going to beat you. And if I can't do it, I will find someone who can!" I glared them down (well, they were taller, so technically I glared them up), and sure enough, to my luck, they apologized, ran off, and never bothered my brother again. I am sure the actual event consisted of me stuttering and them laughing at my attempt at domination, but the memory I have built is that I was the heroine of the story; I faced the bullies, and they fled. I would like to stick with that, thanks. The lesson here was that they were much stronger than I was, so they were not threatened by my stature, but they lost their power because I was not afraid. Bullies will pick on only someone who is afraid of them. As soon as the fear leaves, the game is over. This is the same with panic.

When we fear the tight throat, the chest pains, or the racing heart, we escalate and drive the panic to bully us further. When we face the panic and allow it to rage without our resistance, we are actually sending a message to our brains that we are not afraid of the symptoms anymore. The more we accept the sensations, the sooner our minds assess that these feelings are not a threat.

Our natural reaction to a panic attack is usually to run and hide from it until it passes, just like my sweet twelve-year-old brother did with his school bullies. This is our natural response to immense fear, but it is ineffective because the fear and hiding drive the fear. The way I lessened the panic was to throw on my neon high-tops and chase the bully down the alley. It was about acknowledging the bully and showing it I was not afraid.

How I Faced the Panic Bully

1. **Call it out.** When I felt the sensation of a panic attack coming on, I acknowledged that I was having a panic attack. I even used to shout, "This is a panic attack!" This was my first step. Usually our minds will try to tell us, *Indeed, this is a real heart attack this time!* or *What if this isn't a panic attack? What if I really am dying?* I remember how hard it was to get past those thoughts. It was one of the *bravest* steps I took.

2. **I stopped running from the bully.** Once I established that what I was experiencing was indeed a panic attack, my natural response was always to run, resist, and fight. I forced myself to *not* try to talk myself down from it, or to *not* walk it off, or to *not* try to distract myself with yoga poses and iPhone games. Sure, doing those things eased the panic in the moment, but they did not stop the cycle of continual panic attacks.

3. **I stared the bully down.** As I continued to accept the sensations, they sometimes worsened. I could feel the tight chest intensify, but I learned to be brave and just let it be there. I trembled as I focused and acknowledged the shallow breathing, the dizzy head, and any other crazy symptoms my body tried to manifest. I learned to accept it. I gave it full space to rise and fall and finish its surge.

4. **I stood up to the bully.** As I focused intently on my raging body and mind, my pounding heart, my tightening throat, and the other rude and uninvited symptoms, I learned to do something totally insane! *I willed them to get worse.* I concentrated on each symptom, trying to make the panic heighten. I focused on my throat getting tighter, my chest feeling heavier; and I used my will to make my heart beat faster. If I was trembling, I willed my body to tremble harder. If I was dizzy, I allowed myself to feel dizzy. Have you ever willed dizziness before?! Yeah, neither had I. Doing this showed my mind and body that I was now in charge and that these natural symptoms of panic were empty threats. The bully can charge and threaten you with a bunch of crazy symptoms, but you will not be moved.

5. **Then I watched the bully run.** As I let the wave of symptoms rise and fall, I gave my body total acceptance of what it felt it needed to do to protect me. I learned not to back down, no matter how frightening the symptoms and thoughts became. When the panic attack was over, I told

myself, *I did it*, even if I was able to stand firm for only a few minutes.

The adage "Face your fear" is in full mode here. This is exactly how David fought Goliath. Everyone kept hiding and running from this giant, until finally David had had enough and he shouted back, *"Hey, you don't scare me!"*

It took approximately three days of this technique to stop panic attacks, after four months of daily torture. Stopping panic and anxiety is all about taking your confidence back. It is about taking control of your mind and body again, and learning not to fear the fear. You have *bravery* inside you!

APPLICATION: What is the most distressing panic attack symptom that really gets you panicked (e.g., chest pain, shortness of breath, racing thoughts)? Focus on that one symptom the next time it comes at you and face it. Close your eyes and let it be present.

Day 4

Mornings and Evenings

I am weary with my sighing; every night I make my bed swim, I dissolve my couch with my tears. My eye has wasted away with grief.

—PSALM 6:6–7 NASB

Are you exhausted? I was. I slept sitting up for months, all night long. The anxiety and terror were so intense that I was afraid to sleep, afraid to be off guard, afraid to truly rest. I have made it through five newborns, but this exhaustion was unbearable. As I slept, my dreams were tense, vivid, and my thoughts never stopped. I was always half awake, aware of my thoughts, my body, and my fears. After months of no sleep, despair started creeping in. I would wake up in the morning and my first conscious thought would be panic or deep, despairing depression. I dreaded sleeping. I dreaded waking up.

Today we are going to take back these dreaded mornings and evenings. We are going to end our days victorious and begin our mornings refreshed. We must learn to set the tone for our day. Let me explain why mornings and evenings are our most vulnerable times for anxiety.

Left Brain/Right Brain

Mornings and evenings can be the worst times for anxiety for several reasons. One is a very scientific reason: When we first wake up in the morning, or are just falling asleep, the left brain (our logical side) is the last to wake up and the first to fall asleep. That is why artists and writers recommend writing first thing in the morning or late at night. The right brain (our creative side) is more alert and active during these times.[1] And when the left brain is dragging behind, the imagination goes wild! Don't believe me? When did your best, gushy, dramatic love letters to that junior high crush get written? Three in the afternoon? Doubt it. Just when we are about to fall asleep our emotions and imaginations run wild, and our best soliloquies are written. No wonder our imaginative fears are more heightened during this time as well.

What we are going to learn to do with this is to replace our fearful imaginations and thoughts with good things and take some control back.

Spiritual Weak Spot

Satan can be the thief of our sleep and the tormentor of our days. He goes to great lengths to rob us of our rest and sanity. Daniel 7:25 says, "He [Satan] shall speak words against the Most High, and shall wear out the saints of the Most High" (ESV). Do you feel worn out? I know I did. It is exhausting battling thoughts and facing panic attacks day and night. How can we rest if Satan never rests from trying to derail us? Satan knows that if he can rob us of our sleep, he can rob us of our peace and purpose. When he robs us of our peace and purpose, he robs God. Knowing what we know about how the left brain and right brain function naturally, don't you think Satan can use this as a weak spot?

If we go without rest, we are not as stable the next day, and we become more vulnerable to anxiety and warped thinking. It was the following Scripture that began to release the grip Satan had on my sleep: "In peace I will lie down and sleep, for you alone, Lord, make me dwell in safety" (Psalm 4:8 NIV). This verse was a huge challenge to me, because I was slowly learning to trust God in the day when I could stop and pray. I could relieve some of the thoughts by keeping busy and distracted. But to trust God when I slept, when I had no control over my own protection?! Forget it!

Yet God kept pursuing me through His Word. "Then you will walk in your way securely and your foot will not stumble. When you lie down, you will not be afraid; when you lie down, your sleep will be sweet. Do not be afraid of sudden fear nor of the onslaught of the wicked when it comes" (Proverbs 3:23–25 NASB). He was trying to tell me that He is our protector not just in the day when we have some control, but also in the night when we are defenseless. He is there when the onslaught of fear comes upon us, and He will not let us stumble in it.

David, in the Psalms, speaks much of sleep. Imagine how much terror he would have had to face in the evenings, being pursued by his enemies who were actually trying to kill him. His enemies knew that if they could catch the anointed king asleep he was defenseless, but David needed rest to be able to battle, and he needed to be alert to defend himself. David, like you and me, was tormented with sleepless and fearful nights. David had to get to a point in his walk with God that he entrusted everything to Him: his soul, his mind, his kingdom, and even his sleep.

If we take God at His word, we can have full confidence that He loves us and guards us twenty-four hours a day, without our help. God wants us to prepare for sleep and for waking because it is necessary for our souls and needed for the battle.

Meditating on Your Bed

"My soul is satisfied as with marrow and fatness, and my mouth offers praises with joyful lips. When I remember You on my bed, *I meditate on You in the night watches*, for You have been my help, and in the shadow of Your wings I sing for joy" (Psalm 63:5–7 NASB; emphasis mine). The key to this Scripture is that *meditation upon your bed* leads to healing and security. This was an important part of my spiritual and mental healing. I began to meditate on the goodness of God, on beautiful things and hopeful things, before I fell asleep each night. As I developed this habit, my sleep and my days began to change. We will cover this concept of meditation in greater detail on Day 9, but for now I want to focus on making sure that we start the day and end the day in the best way possible.

Morning and Evening Declarations

As much as I dreaded sleep during this time, the mornings were sometimes unbearable. I woke up one morning with the darkest despair I had ever felt. And it terrified me. It was as if the enemy wanted first dibs on my morning. If he could derail me before God could encourage me, then he knew I would spend the rest of my day in fear, rattled by his intimidating taunts. Every morning after a rough sleep, I would list in my head all the things I had to conquer that day, and I built my anxiety on worrying about how I was going to cope.

We already make morning declarations whether we realize it or not—declarations like "Today is going to be hard; I feel exhausted"; or "I'm going to have a horrible day, because I had a horrible sleep!"; or "I'm tired and anxious and the day hasn't even started." You have already prophesied your day into existence without even knowing it.

I began to take my mornings back by declaring my thoughts, every morning—something I adopted from Joyce Meyer. It is quite simple. Simply declare out loud before your feet even touch the carpet the kind of day you will have. I began to declare my healing, my freedom, and my blessings every morning, whether I believed them or not. As I began to take my mornings back, I truly began to see greater freedom throughout my day. It was powerful. I would sit up in bed, anxious or not, and say out loud:

I am blessed.
My children are blessed.

My home is blessed.

My health is blessed.

My husband is blessed.

My spirit is awake.

My soul is saved.

My mind is sound.

My future is good.

At first I did not believe what I was saying. Each thing I said seemed religious and without feeling, but as I continued, my spirit began to believe it, and soon my mind did as well. When we speak life over ourselves, it breaks the curse of darkness and allows little room for Satan's influence. The Lord says, "Death and life are in the power of the tongue, and those who love it will eat its fruits" (Proverbs 18:21 ESV).

Anxiety wasn't the only thing keeping me from rest. Severe depression was creeping in as well. Extreme hopelessness had choked me, and my thoughts were far from healthy and sane. I could battle the thoughts during the day, with Scripture, prayer, and distraction. However, some nights my thoughts took over even as I drifted to sleep.

Within days of implementing my morning and evening declarations, I began to feel the cloud lift, and my thoughts automatically began to turn to good things, to positive statements versus despairing, anxious thoughts. I was having victory over my sleep once again. Then one evening, something amazing happened, something that proved to me that God truly does guard our sleep.

I had been reading my Bible and pondering what God was

saying, when I began to doze off. Soon my thoughts that I had set on God began subconsciously drifting back toward depression, self-loathing, and despair. I remember the feeling of "Woe is me" as I dreamed, when all of a sudden, I was jolted awake by an audible voice: "Stop it!" I was shaken out of my negative thoughts as if a bucket of ice water had been dashed in my face. I sat straight up. As my thoughts began to drift back toward bondage, God intervened. I believe the Holy Spirit—who had been leading me to victory in the night—was on guard.

That was the last night I was attacked in my sleep. I had such a profound glimpse into God's character that I was forever changed. The Shepherd never sleeps when guarding His flock. He does not grow weary of protecting us. He truly will never leave us or forsake us.

APPLICATION: Take a moment to pray and reflect on your blessings. Write out ten declarations that you can speak over yourself daily.

Day 5

Guilt-Free Rest

❦

Truly my soul finds rest in God;
  my salvation comes from him.
Truly he is my rock and my salvation;
  he is my fortress, I will never be shaken.

—PSALM 62:1–2 NIV

May I make an educated guess that by nature you are the push-through, feel-the-burn kind of person with a habit of biting off more than you can chew? Am I right? If I am, you fit in with the vast majority of those who fall into anxiety. Today's topic of rest may be a challenge for you, especially the guilt-free part. However, you must learn to experience the *rest of God*, because this will be the turnaround lesson for you. This is where God can begin the deeper work because you are finally sitting still long enough for Him to get done what He needs to do. Chances are unrest got you into this mess, and so resting is what will get you out.

Burnout

The first warning that I was about to break down was in the form of burnout. My body just kind of shut down. I was physically exhausted all the time, I was numb emotionally, and I was lifeless spiritually. Burnout is just what it sounds like: The light just goes out. Most of us never see it coming, though I am sure, if you are anything like I was, you have had people try to hint, with comments like, "Are you sure that's not too much?" To which we respond, "No, I like being busy." Or maybe you noticed emotional meltdowns on Sundays when your week came to a halt. Or perhaps your health had been telling you all along.

With my fifth newborn in tow, I volunteered to help a team revamp the entire Sunday school. It was intense, and it took all of my resources, time, creativity, and more. At first it was an energy high because I was fueled with vision; I love creating and being a leader, and I also knew that God was calling me to it. But there was one condition—I was to build it up and then pass it on. I felt very strongly that God told me, *Six months. You build this project in six months and then you're out.*

When the six months passed, it seemed that this project was just getting started. I knew pulling out would cause a very big strain on everyone else, yet I sensed a strong warning from God. I brought my thoughts to the leaders, and to be honest I could tell they were annoyed. I felt like they saw me as flaky or unreliable. "You have to count the cost," they said. "You can't just start something and then quit." They were right in the black-and-white reality of life. I was conflicted; I hated people disapproving of me. And then I did what every "good" Christian woman does: I chose the approval of man over God's instruction. I was wrong for letting fear of disappointing man overshadow God's command.

I pushed past the six-month mark, and then, just one disobedient month later, I crashed and burned. *Hard.* I was completely disabled. The light inside of me—physically, emotionally, and even spiritually—just went out. I was physically exhausted all the time, I was crying at anything, and I was completely numb at the same time. I had nothing left for anyone, and it happened quickly.

My going from being an overachiever to not even being able to get dressed in the morning was a shock to my family and to me. God—so gracious to restore where I messed up—began speaking to me about resting in Him. He really wanted me to know it, because everywhere I turned He spoke to me about it. I would email a friend to ask for prayer, and my friend would tell me the Lord wanted me to rest. Someone whom I hadn't talked to in months sent me a Bible verse—the central theme was rest. I would get a phone call out of the blue and would hear, "I have been praying for you and I feel the Lord is telling me you need to rest."

I get it, God. You want me to rest!

But how could I? I had a ministry and five children, including a newborn and a teenager. I had volunteer duties, functions to attend, deadlines to meet, people to impress, and rejection to avoid. Oh, and a blog! *I'll rest later* is what I told God.

Well, He knows better than we do, doesn't He? I didn't listen—again—and soon enough I was forced into rest, thanks to a complete and final mental breakdown. First burnout, then depression, and then anxiety.

In *The Rest of God: Restoring Your Soul by Restoring Sabbath,* Mark Buchanan wrote that busyness kills the heart:

> One measure of whether or not you're rested enough—besides falling asleep in board meetings—is to ask yourself this: *How much do I care about the things I care about?* When we lose concern for people, both the lost and the found, for the bride of Christ, for friendship, for truth and beauty and goodness; when we cease to laugh (and instead yell at people to quiet down) or to weep when our spouses weep (and instead wish they didn't get so emotional); when we hear the news of trouble among our neighbors and our first thought is that we hope it isn't going to involve us; when we stop caring about the things we care about—that's the signal we're too busy. This is all the byproduct of being consumed by the things that feed the ego but starve the soul. Busyness kills the heart.[1]

That burnout, which starved my soul, was more than five years ago; and that burnout, coupled with my continued disobedience to rest, is what led me right into panic, anxiety, and depression. It took me several years to recover—a time I can never get back. Through God's leading and my desperate need to heal, I learned how to rest. It wasn't as simple as putting my feet up. I had to labor through some stubborn mind-sets and some of the deep heart issues that kept me from resting in the first place—pride, perfectionism, insecurity, fear of man, ego. It was work worth doing because rest healed my heart.

What Does It Mean to Rest?

Imagine you have a broken foot. You are told to wear a boot and use crutches so that you don't put pressure on the injury. Then once everything is stabilized, you have to elevate the leg and rest it as much as possible.

When you break your foot and are given these instructions, your life will *not* resume as normal. You will have to opt out of your spin class, turn down the request to carpool kids on their ski trip, and you may even have to ask your kids or hubby to get the mail each day and walk the dog. If you try to rush the process, your foot will not heal and you will risk injuring yourself further.

You get the metaphor. The same applies to your mental health. If something in you is broken, then you need rest to heal.

To be honest, I had no idea where to begin this new call to rest. In total humility I called the two friends I knew would tell me the truth no matter how hard it was to hear. I made coffee and welcomed them in for my self-declared Rest Intervention. "Bear one another's burdens, and so fulfill the law of Christ" (Galatians 6:2 ESV). I wrote down a list—a very long list—of all my current responsibilities and commitments. When they walked through the door and sat next to me on my red couch, I unrolled the list like a royal messenger and begged them to help me purge it. One by one, we dissected what was necessary in my life and what had been taken on as a result of unhealthy excuses. My friends helped me to break down each item on the list and express my true motive behind agreeing to do them all. Was it guilt, pride, fear? Any commitment on my list that was motived by guilt, pride, or fear was a big fat "CROSS OFF THE LIST."

Learning to rest, for me, was learning to understand why I had taken on what I had. It was also important for me to understand that rest was not just physical rest. It was also emotional, mental, and spiritual rest. It did not encompass just sleep or taking a breather to check Facebook or to Bejewel my heart out. True rest meant taking time aside to breathe in God's creation and walk with Him. It involved releasing my emotions to the Lord and giving Him all of my burdens. It was acknowledging all of my worries and my to-do lists and then asking God to take over.

What Is Rest?

- Knowing that He is God and we are His children—this is rest.

- Taking time to let things go and give them over to Him to deal with—this is rest.

- Knowing that we do not need to strive to be approved by God—this is rest.

You won't always need to be this guarded, but for this season it is absolutely necessary that you endure the least amount of stress—physically, emotionally, and spiritually.

Resting in Obedience to God

We think we can outwork God. Sometimes we even think we are so important that if we say no to something, the world will crumble. We all know God rested from His works on the seventh day, but we make our lives way too important for that. A lot of our *doing* is our way of controlling our anxiety. Only if we do it ourselves can we know it will be done right. Right?

> On the seventh day God finished his work that he had done, and he rested on the seventh day from all his work that he had done. So God blessed the seventh day and made it holy, because on it God rested from all his work that he had done in creation.
>
> GENESIS 2:2–3 ESV

When the Israelites were slaves in Egypt, God saw their bondage and desired for them to be free. His only requirement of them was to rest in Him. God never said, "I am freeing you from bondage so that you can serve Me, work hard, be perfect, and strive for My love." That is exactly what He was trying to save them from! God said He was freeing them from the hard bondage they were forced to serve so they would know that "they will be my people, and I will be their God" (Jeremiah 32:38 NIV). But the people would not have it, and they refused the rest God had for them. And they paid the consequences for it: "Let us, therefore, make every effort to enter that rest, so that no one will perish by following their example of disobedience" (Hebrews 4:11 NIV).

Do not be like the Israelites here; stop resisting the rest that God is trying to offer you. He knows you are in a tough season. He knows you are broken. He knows you are weak. He expects nothing from you. He has come to take you out of bondage. Trust Him. He will tell you when it is time to get up and move on.

We love to strive, don't we? We are always trying to gain the approval of man and to control our circumstances, just like the Israelites. When we feel God isn't moving fast enough, we build our own gods and try to work out our own problems. But I am here to tell you that the warning in Hebrews is a word for us today. We are to make every effort to enter His rest.

I know that if we truly grasped the obedience of rest, we would be happier, healthier, and holier. Our families would be stronger, and our marriages, too. I think we would hear from God more, find contentment more, and actually accomplish more. God has a rest for you and me that is available to those who seek it and ask for it. It was the key to the Promised Land for the Israelites, and it will be the key to yours as well.

⤜⤏

APPLICATION: Resting does not always mean sleeping; we can feel refreshed when we go for a walk, read a book, or paint. Write out three activities that refuel you. Then find time in your schedule to add these back into your life each week.

Day 6

Words of Power

～✦～

Speech is the mirror of the soul; as a man speaks, so he is.

—PUBLILIUS SYRUS

I had never been so fascinated as I was by a YouTube video on rice.[1] A man took three glass jars and filled each jar with half a cup of cooked rice. Several times a day this man would interact with the three jars of rice in a different way. He spoke hateful words to the first jar of rice—cursing the rice, insulting it, and just being all-out rude. He completely neglected the second jar of rice. He did not look at it or speak to it. To the third cup of rice, this man spoke words of love, encouragement, kindness, and good things. In just a few weeks something astounding began to take place. The first jar of rice, the hated one, rotted. Mold filled the rice and the stench was strong. The second jar of rice, the ignored rice, turned completely black and hardened. The final jar, the loved jar of rice, had fermented into a sweet-smelling rice wine. Crazy, isn't it?

I remember watching this and thinking how destructive our words can be to children and can ultimately affect how they turn out. I believe that how a child is spoken to is often how a child matures. Are they cold and hardened after years of neglect, toxic and angry after years of abuse, or sweet and productive after a life of love and encouragement? The video was a powerful visual of how our words can bring life or death.

Words Have Power

Jesus showed this truth through His words when He cursed the fig tree and it died:

> Seeing in the distance a fig tree in leaf, he went to find out if it had any fruit. When he reached it, he found nothing but leaves, because it was not the season for figs. Then he said to the tree, "May no one ever eat fruit from you again." And his disciples heard him say it... In the morning, as they went along, they saw the fig tree withered from the roots. Peter remembered and said to Jesus, "Rabbi, look! The fig tree you cursed has withered!"
>
> MARK 11:13–14, 20–21 NIV

Jesus, of course, also used His words to heal, to encourage, and to forgive. He set many people free with His words, and He gave us the same power to curse or bless with the words we speak. In this same story Jesus taught about how much power we have in our words when we have the faith behind them:

> "Have faith in God," Jesus answered. "Truly I tell you, if anyone says to this mountain, 'Go, throw yourself into the sea,' and does not doubt in their heart but believes that what they say will happen, it will be done for them.

Therefore I tell you, whatever you ask for in prayer, believe that you have received it, and it will be yours. And when you stand praying, if you hold anything against anyone, forgive them, so that your Father in heaven may forgive you your sins."

MARK 11:22–25 NIV

Today, we have some mountains we need to speak to! If there were a magic word you could quote to lift the anxiety assaults that come your way, I am sure you would be less fearful. Often, our best-intentioned loved ones will say things like "Can't you just tell yourself it's not true when a fearful thought comes?" or my favorite, "Just don't think about it, then." What they do not understand is how completely overwhelmed our minds are to be able to handle any rational thought, let alone talk ourselves out of the irrational thought. A fearful paralysis seems to take over and we get stuck in our minds, unable to move from the topic we are most fearful of. I had many dear friends tell me that the next time I had an anxiety attack I should call them. It was sweet but hard to follow through, because when an attack came, I was mentally and physically cemented.

Words can have self-defining power over our lives and over the thoughts we have. They can bring life or they can bring death. I remember sharing with a friend how bad my anxiety was, and in her attempt to make me feel better, she said to me, "You don't look near as bad as my friend who ended up killing herself." She saw the look on my face when she said that and begged her words back, but it was too late. The fear of becoming suicidal gripped me. For months pictures of news headlines popped into my mind: "Mother of Five Drives Off Bridge, Leaving Her Grieving Family Behind." I became afraid of anything I could use to harm myself, and nothing I could say to myself was going to erase the fear. My friend never meant to cause this fear. But it shows how powerful our words are. If words can be that powerful against us, then good words must have equal or greater power to break strongholds and demolish fears. "Anxiety in the heart of man causes depression, but a good word makes it glad" (Proverbs 12:25 NKJV). It is true that those who struggle with anxiety usually are led into depression. But what I love about this Scripture is the truth that a good word can heal anxiety.

Emergency Cue Cards

In a real life-and-death emergency you call 911. As soon as you are on the phone with the dispatcher, you are instructed to stay on the line. The dispatcher's job is to assess the situation, keep you calm, and assist by giving lifesaving advice. Today is about getting you through those mental emergencies, those days you feel jagged, and the moments when you are sideswiped with fear by creating your own mental health emergency responder. It's for those public moments when you are overcome with anxiety in the middle of a meeting, or out with friends, or shopping in crowds. In the middle of what I call a mental emergency—a moment of extreme panic, a dark depression, or an obsessive fear—it may not be appropriate to call 911, but you can reach into your pocket and pull out your Emergency Cue Card.

A cue card is a piece of paper with your power words already written out. It will be written by you, specifically for you, with your own words of promise and encouragement. Whatever you hope someone would say to you in a moment of panic instead of "Just calm down," you will say to yourself on this card. Whatever promises you need to be reminded of in the moment of hopelessness, they are there. Any Scriptures that you cling to, or events you look forward to, they're all written out for you to read.

MY EMERGENCY CUE CARD
THIS WILL PASS   I WILL FEEL BETTER IN 15 MINUTES

My Thoughts ARE NOT my truth

I SURVIVED THE LAST ONE, I WILL GET THROUGH THIS ONE TOO

God's plan for my life is to prosper me, not to harm me

I am not alone and I am deeply loved

I'VE HAD PANIC ATTACKS BEFORE AND I GOT THROUGH THOSE TOO

I'm stronger than I think I am

God, I lay all my anxieties down before You, knowing that You see them all and have conquered them all

---

When we are frozen from a mind onslaught, we can simply pull out our cue cards and read them, over and over, drowning out the tormenting thoughts, replacing harmful thoughts with loving thoughts, speaking encouragement where we are discouraged. The more we read the words in our moment of despair, the more we can speak to the mountain of anxiety and tell it to move.

This is going to help you immensely in the short term, but what is so powerful about this technique is that every time you pull out your emergency cue card and speak or read the words, it becomes an act of spiritual warfare! You begin to do exactly what the Word of God says:

> We demolish arguments and every pretension that sets itself up against the knowledge of God, and we take captive every thought to make it obedient to Christ.
>
> 2 CORINTHIANS 10:5 NIV

I still have my card. It is ratty and the text is barely visible now. I used to pull it out often, anywhere and at any time. It has carried me through some pretty rough moments. At the very top, in bold letters, it reads "THIS WILL PASS." I meant it, in the short term and in the long term. My card was right. It did pass. Every anxiety attack, every despairing thought, every harmful thought, every panic attack—it passed and I got through it. Then, eventually, my season of anguish passed, too. I once had a student in my online course who had such an intense bout of anxiety and depression that she transferred her cue card onto a giant whiteboard and kept it by her front door. Whatever your card looks like, the purpose is to surround yourself with truth.

Surround Yourself with Good Words

Now that you know how much power words have, it is very important that you surround yourself with love, affirmation, and peace. You just may not be able to watch the news anymore or binge-watch Netflix dramas. You may, for a season, have to avoid Aunt Jo-Jo and her health-care rants, and you may need to replace watching *Criminal Minds* with watching a funny sitcom. It is important that you surround yourself with good, with joy, with words of life. We have grown accustomed to garbage in our culture, just like our food. Our entertainment is over-consumed and bad for our health. We need to be more aware of our environments and what we are listening to.

Before we end today, I want to encourage you with some life-giving words:

- You will not be like this forever.

- This will pass, and you will look back on this season in your life with a mixture of sorrow and deep thankful-ness, because the fire in you is producing precious stones. I promise! The journey reshaped me and changed me for-ever, for the good and for God's glory.

- You are stronger than you think, and God has placed His Spirit in you! He looks at you with total adoration and longs to see you free.

- You can do this; I know you can!

⤬

APPLICATION: Take some time to pray and ponder
on the words that you know you will need to hear in
times of mental assaults. Go through old journals, find
underlined Bible verses, greeting cards from loved ones,
or new promises God has spoken over your life. Choose
the words that bring you hope and peace, and write
them on your card.

Day 7

Befriending Anxiety

❧

I must not fear. Fear is the mind-killer. Fear is the little death that brings total obliteration. I will face my fear. I will permit it to pass over me and through me. And when it has gone past I will turn the inner eye to see its path. Where the fear has gone there will be nothing. Only I will remain.

—FRANK HERBERT

I have a friend whose name is "Anxious Annie." She is a very good friend, and I can't imagine life without her. She is always helping me to stay out of trouble and reminds me of all the things I have to get done. She helps me meet deadlines, she helps me stay on task, and she always makes sure I am making wise decisions. Lately, though, she comes around *all* the time, and it's getting annoying. She talks too much, complains too much, and freaks out over everything! I try to get things done, but she just demands too much of my energy and time and never leaves me alone. Ignoring her doesn't work, and yelling at her to go away doesn't work. If I try to drown her out, the next day she pouts and is even more demanding! I don't want to lose her as a friend, but she is seriously in need of some boundaries.

Meet My Friend Anxiety

We know from Day 1 that fear is necessary to keep us protected and to help us act fast when we are in a harmful situation. However, when anxiety begins to rule our lives, bombard our thoughts, and wear down our bodies, we must begin to regain some control again and take back our lives. I tried meditating on God, calming music, breathing techniques, ignoring the anxiety, distracting myself, even cold showers. Some worked in the moment, but nothing put anxiety in its place like befriending it did.

During the beginning stages of my breakdown, I was sent to an internal medicine specialist who did a thorough checkup to make sure there were no other underlying health issues causing anxiety-like symptoms. The doctor must have seen hundreds of patients like me—convinced we are dying, yet perfectly healthy—and he knew how to gently tell me that this was *all* anxiety! It was a reality check for me. I almost wished I had some other medical problem, because then I could blame that. But I had to accept the fact that I, this supermom, ministry leader, how-do-you-do-it-all blogger, and life of the party, was indeed suffering from a mental breakdown. The doctor was kind and compassionate, and he gave me some advice on stress-management techniques. Then he said, "Give your anxiety a name, like Debbie, treat it like a friend; don't fight it; just welcome it."

I can't say that in my life I have ever had a friend who brought on feelings of uneasiness, total panic, obsessive worry, repetitive thoughts, problems sleeping, cold or sweaty hands, shortness of breath, heart palpitations, an inability to be still and calm, dry mouth, numbness or tingling in my hands or feet, nausea, fear of going crazy, fear of hurting myself or others, muscle tension, and total fear! Who wants that kind of friend around? Sheesh, send her home and block her on Facebook!

What the doctor said, though, was right. Befriending my anxiety was the most effective way to put anxiety back into its rightful place. The fundamental idea is not to try to rid yourself of anxiety or battle it, but to accept it. The more you befriend it, and the kinder you are to it, the sooner it will calm down.

This is very similar to how we dealt with the panic bully. The only difference here is that with general anxiety we do not confront it and will it to get worse—we befriend it. It is important that we do not turn against ourselves when dealing with anxiety. Anxiety truly is your friend; it is a part of you, designed to protect you and keep you from harm. Our fear response is not evil; it is just not functioning in the way it was created. What happens when we resist and fight anxiety? We begin an internal struggle we will never win. We feel anxiety coming on, and we think we are flawed; then we panic. *What's wrong with me?* we ask. We begin to lose confidence, wondering if we have any control over our thoughts at all. It is a vicious cycle that tragically can keep people trapped in anxiety for a lifetime.

I'm reminded of our little puppy that we brought home to the kids many years ago. What started off as the most adorable little furball turned into a full-grown little shih tzu named Winston. That dog was unpredictable; anytime a robin would land in the yard it would go crazy; anytime a person would walk by or a box rolled into the yard from a windstorm, this dog lost it. The dog had so much anxiety that it broke its knee, not once but twice, by bolting off the couch to bark at a passing dog. I remember hearing a dog psychologist say that when we yell at dogs to stop them from barking, it only encourages the behavior and adds to their anxiety. When you speak calmly and stand with the dog, it eases their anxiety and therefore eases the barking. Your anxiety is not the rottweiler you fear it is. Think of it as an overactive shih tzu limping off the couch. We need to fully accept our anxiety and befriend it.

I was the perfect example of someone who fueled her anxiety with thoughts about the anxiety. Whenever an anxiety attack would come on strong, I would tense up and say to myself, *Oh, no! It's back!* and my thoughts would cycle into a pattern of *What if it stays forever?* Or *What's happening to me?* Or *How am I going to function today, when I am shaking uncontrollably?* In my mind, I was trying to come to terms with what I was thinking and feeling; I was trying to grasp some control and solve the problem. But what I was left with was an even greater sense of doom. When I began implementing the idea of befriending "Annie," I was still very aware of the physical sensations, the thoughts and the fears, which did not lessen at first, but I learned to allow them to come, and stay, and heighten, and surge, and then disappear.

However new or strange the symptoms, or however intense the thoughts, I did my best to allow them to come without resistance. By accepting and welcoming the anxiety, I lessened the tension brought on by fighting against it. And the more I welcomed it, the less powerful it became. Soon I was becoming more confident in handling my anxiety, and soon that confidence led me to being able to get on with my day without it crippling me. That led to the anxiety leaving altogether. One day I realized that I hadn't been anxious for at least three hours, and I celebrated. Then a few days later it was half a day, and I celebrated. Then it was a whole day! Then a few good days, then good weeks!

When anxiety shows up at the door of your mind, you should respond with a polite welcome. It may seem silly, but give it a name. It may seem contrary to your natural instinct to fight anxiety off or ignore it, but you are going to learn to enjoy its presence and welcome it with open arms when it comes. Instead of begrudgingly muttering, "Oh, you're back," you will rather politely greet it with, "Hi, Anxious Annie, I am glad you could show up today to help me bake my kid's birthday cake." Soon the feeling of anxiety that comes will be familiar and friendly. It's not perceived in your subconscious as a threat or an attack, so the intense subconscious reaction to your anxiety is decreased.

Just to clarify, anxiety can bring people to such a desperate place that they will do anything to break free, for example, cutting, high-risk behaviors, acts of rebellion, or substance abuse. This is never okay, and if you find yourself this desperate for relief from anxiety, please seek professional help immediately.

Finding Joy in the Storm

I began using humor a lot when I was overcome with anxious thoughts and symptoms. There is something about not taking yourself so seriously all the time that eases the intensity of anxiety. We have to learn not to let our emotions and thoughts dictate our actions. Just because we feel it does not mean that we must act on it. Just because we think it does not make it true. We must learn to find joy and humor even in the storms. We can rejoice and be glad because we know that God has gone before us and is on our side. "I have set the LORD continually before me; because He is at my right hand, I will not be shaken. Therefore my heart is glad and my glory rejoices; my flesh also will dwell securely" (Psalm 16:8–9 NASB).

❧

APPLICATION: Plan ahead for your next anxious moment. How will you respond? How will you speak to your anxiety? What will you call your new friend? Write out your anxiety plan so you feel prepared.

Day 8

Depersonalization

❧

You cannot make yourself feel something you do not feel, but you can make yourself do right in spite of your feelings.

—PEARL S. BUCK, "MY NEIGHBOR'S SON,"
TO MY DAUGHTERS, WITH LOVE

Anxiety can be a very complex issue, with very odd symptoms and sensations. Some people suffer with only a few symptoms, like fatigue or stuttering. Me, I'm pretty sure I have had every one.

I suffered the strangest symptoms. I would google anxiety symptoms and think, *Oh, thank goodness I don't have* that *symptom*. And then a week later, *BAM!*, I had that symptom. I stuttered, I forgot my own name, I had skin irritations and dry mouth, my legs would go numb, I feared I was going crazy, my stomach was irritable, and I had trouble sleeping. I had clammy hands. I trembled like an old cat. I had constant nightmares and trouble concentrating. I had stomachaches, joint pain, headaches, and dizziness. I felt faint all the time and exhausted. I could go on and on *and on*, but I won't—I don't want to make you anxious!

However, one of the most unsettling symptoms I struggled with was depersonalization—a feeling of being disconnected from myself, a feeling of being *overaware* of myself and of my surroundings, almost an out-of-body feeling. This depersonalization, though not a danger or a sign of a worsening mental condition, was very distressing. A person struggling with depersonalization feels every physical sensation his or her body is having. Your blinking is conscious, your breathing is conscious, even the awareness of your own heartbeat, your own voice, or even your own behaviors. Environments become amplified, sounds stand out, the ticking of a clock becomes rhythmic and amplified. Smells become more intense, patterns become more vibrant—not necessarily in a good way—and soon you lose being a participant in life and become instead a self-critical, anxious observer. It's a horrible sensation.

The sad part about this floating-outside-yourself kind of feeling is the disconnection it causes between you and others. It is hard to be in the moment when you feel this way. It's hard to engage fully with others when you are overaware of yourself, right down to your breath and eyelashes.

This is one of those symptoms that will resolve as you deal with your anxiety as a whole, but I did find five things very helpful in dealing with depersonalization, and I want to share them with you:

Five Tips That Helped Me Reduce Depersonalization

1. **Be encouraged and have peace—this will go away over time.** It is a lingering symptom of your anxiety, but you won't feel it forever. Try not to feel concerned that this means you are going crazy or losing reality. It's these

types of symptoms that I learned to befriend. Nothing is forever, and soon this unsettling feeling will be a thing of the past, another mountain you climbed. "And let us not grow weary of doing good, for in due season we will reap, if we do not give up" (Galatians 6:9 ESV).

2. **Pinch yourself—no, this is not a dream!** When I was overcome with depersonalization, sometimes I just needed to pull out the old Hollywood Scarlett O'Hara slap and tell myself to snap out of it! Once I was so badly disengaged that I thought I would float out of my body at any second and view myself from above. I was desperate for relief. I walked outside in the snow barefoot just to snap out of it. What?! I talk to imaginary friends and go barefoot in the snow?! Wait, don't stop reading! You may be thinking I am a crazy Canadian, but when I needed immediate relief from the symptoms, *it worked*. A splash of cold water, a loud dance song, a jump on the trampoline, a cartwheel in the yard, a sour candy (not a box of them), a squeeze of lemon, a brisk walk—whatever I could do to safely give myself a quick pick-me-up and a jolt helped.

3. **Talk with someone.** I got relief when I was engaged in an in-depth conversation with someone. I found that talking, listening, and being with someone I could engage with helped me to forget my awareness.

4. **Pick up a hobby that requires attention to detail.** Knitting, cross-stitching, woodwork, model trains are all tasks that use your hands and your concentration. Keeping my

mind busy with other things was a great way to check back into reality—not to mention the killing I could have made at the local craft fair. Keeping your mind busy gives you a break from yourself and your anxious thoughts.

5. **Talk with yourself.** What I was experiencing was a normal reaction to extreme stress and anxiety, so I told myself: *Sarah, what you are experiencing is a normal reaction.* When Anxious Annie came to visit, I greeted her out loud: "How's the view from up there, Annie?" I learned not to take myself too seriously; humor and self-talk reduced the anxiety I was feeling in relation to my extreme symptoms. This was also a great time to use my emergency cue card!

Remember that your body will throw the strangest and newest symptoms at you periodically when you are dealing with anxiety. It's like the little child who tests her parents' boundaries for her own security. Your mind and body do the same. Expect some victories and setbacks along the way; it is all part of the process.

❦

APPLICATION: Follow the five steps to break free from this cycle of feeling disconnected. Keep a practice of befriending your anxiety and treat this symptom in a similar way.

Biblical Meditation

*In the silence of the heart God speaks. If you face God in prayer
and silence, God will speak to you. Then you will know that
you are nothing. It is only when you realize your nothingness,
your emptiness, that God can fill you with Himself. Souls of
prayer are souls of great silence.*

—MOTHER TERESA, *IN THE HEART OF THE WORLD*

If I had to pick the most important subject, this would probably
be at the top of the list. We have talked a lot in previous chapters about symptoms and how to handle panic attacks, anxiety,
and depersonalization. These are all great ways to deal with
the symptoms and ease the torment of anxiety, but that's not
enough. We want total healing. It is now time to start going a
little deeper—to start pulling weeds and building up the broken places.

If you are reading this and you are not a Christian, that's
okay. Healing is just as available to you through the techniques
I am showing you, but sometimes when we go through seasons
like the one you are in, we need something greater, something
bigger than our humanity to pull us the rest of the way out. It
is that hand reaching out that pulls us to standing. If it weren't
for God leading me out, I would still be lost in my fears, coping

maybe, but lost. You can have this same hope! Open your heart to the idea that there is more healing, more wholeness, more joy, and a bigger future for you than you can imagine. Bear with me, and trust that what I am showing you is not religion, but food for your soul.

What Is Biblical Meditation?

God intended meditation to be a moment of communion between Him and us. The Bible clearly speaks of it often: "Let the words of my mouth and the meditation of my heart be acceptable in Your sight, O LORD, my rock and my Redeemer" (Psalm 19:14 NASB). However, there is a very distinct difference between biblical meditation, New Age meditation, and Eastern religion meditation. Before we begin, it is very important that we understand the difference between them. One has the power to strengthen your spirit and renew your mind, and the others can be an open door to bondage.

Mantra meditation is one example of many practices of meditation taught throughout the world, especially to those struggling with anxiety. It is very commonly recommended to those struggling with mental illness. The idea is to drown out anxious thoughts by repeating a phrase or word until you feel calm.

Yoga is another popular form of meditation, meaning "yoked to the divine," and was created to bring one closer to the spirit realm called *Brahman*, which in essence is the spirit realm of nothingness. Another practice commonly used in various forms of meditation is the cross-legged posture and "ohm" chanting that was created to unite oneself with one's "inner god." Other forms of meditation include Zen meditation, Chakra, self-affirmation meditation, and reflective meditation.

It is important that we truly understand what other forms of meditation there are in order to be discerning in what we open our fragile minds to. These listed forms of meditation should never be sought after as a Christian. Romans 12:1–2 (NIV) says, "Therefore, I urge you, brothers and sisters, in view of God's mercy, to offer your bodies as a living sacrifice, holy and pleasing to God—this is your true and proper worship. Do not conform to the pattern of this world, but be transformed by the renewing of your mind. Then you will be able to test and approve what God's will is—his good, pleasing and perfect will." We are to offer our bodies—and minds—holy before God. This Scripture also urges us to avoid conforming to the world's way of thinking and not to empty our minds, but to test them, transform them, and renew them.

Now that I have made you run scared from the idea of meditation, I am going to reintroduce you to the biblical concept of meditation that is pleasing to God and effective in renewing your mind. Meditation belongs to God and will be one of the most powerful tools in healing your mind. Again, biblical meditation is not about emptying your mind, but rather about filling it with God's Word and listening to His heart. It is about focusing on a part of Scripture and remembering God's goodness in your life. Biblical meditation is not about detaching yourself from your life, but about attaching yourself to the living God. As Irving L. Jensen so aptly says in *How to Profit from Bible Reading,* "Reflection is the mind and heart at work, thinking over and concentrating on what the eyes have seen... Reflection in Bible reading should have the intensity of meditation, whereby the soul has the desire and intention of obeying God's Word."

Biblical meditation is not about reflecting on yourself and your own strengths, but about reflecting on God's strength. Do you see the difference?

Whether we sit cross-legged, inhale deeply, and close our eyes is insignificant. It is our hearts and our focus that separate worldly meditation from biblical meditation. If we do not learn to take meditation back for ourselves as a daily discipline, we miss out on something very restorative and necessary for our overall spiritual and mental health.

How to Meditate

Biblical meditation has three elements: remembrance, listening, and pondering. It can be a set-aside time of prayer and reflection, or thinking on a certain aspect of God or Scripture throughout the day, or sitting in silence waiting upon God to speak. I often hear people say that they don't need to stop and pray to God—that they talk to Him all day. I think that talking to God all day is amazing, and we are called to think of Him often and go to Him at any time of day, with anything on our hearts. However, there is something much deeper and richer in setting time aside to stop and meditate on God, to pray, to listen, and to just sit in silence.

Remembrance. "When I remember You on my bed, I meditate on You in the night watches" (Psalm 63:6 NASB). Quieting yourself to reflect and remember all that God is, all He has done, and what He says He will do is meditation. This is especially effective for anxiety when you can reflect on all the times you were anxious and God brought peace, or the time you feared the unknown and it all turned out fine. "I will meditate on all Your work and muse on Your deeds" (Psalm 77:12 NASB). Keep bringing your thoughts back to remembering what He has done and, most importantly, who He says He is. Remember the first time you felt His presence or the first time you accepted Him into your life. Remembering God has a powerful way of filling the future with hope, because we have seen God work out our trials many times before.

Listening. God has more thoughts toward us than we can count, and He longs to share them with us. "How precious also are Your thoughts to me, O God! How great is the sum of them! If I should count them, they would be more in number than the sand; when I awake, I am still with You" (Psalm 139:17–18 NKJV). You would be forever surprised how loving and patient His thoughts are toward us—way more loving and forgiving than the thoughts we have toward ourselves. Disciplining ourselves away from our own thoughts to meditate and focus on His thoughts can connect us to God in a greater way. " 'For my thoughts are not your thoughts, neither are your ways my ways,' declares the LORD. 'As the heavens are higher than the earth, so are my ways higher than your ways and my thoughts than your thoughts'" (Isaiah 55:8–9 NIV). I look back over my journals of my relationship with God where I have written out my heart toward Him, and then listened and recorded what I felt He was speaking back to me. There have been rich, defining moments as I listened to hear God. Whether it was in a verse or in that still, small voice that comes with a flood of peace, joy, and pure emotion, I listened. Our God loves us. He really, really loves us. He longs to commune with us, He longs to hear our voices, and He longs to share His heart, too. Six months of therapy could not compare to one single encouragement from God Himself. Eventually, as I began to listen for God's heart, I was more able to adopt His thoughts toward others and myself. Anxiety has a hard time finding room in your mind when God's thoughts are cleaning house with His affirmations toward you!

Pondering. I chose the word "pondering" because it reminds me of Mary, pondering the promise of Jesus to come. "But Mary treasured up all these things and pondered them in her heart" (Luke 2:19 NIV). When we meditate, we ponder the Word of God, His prophecies, His promises, and His character. "I will meditate on Your precepts and regard Your ways. I shall delight in Your statutes; I shall not forget Your word" (Psalm

119:15–16 NASB). I can only imagine the anxiety Mary must have felt knowing she was raising the Messiah. Pondering the promises of God over herself and her son gave her great strength and helped her to stay focused on her role in the great redemption of the world. Spending the day pondering God's promises over us, or pondering His character, will turn our daily focus onto Him and off of our fear. It turns our worship back toward Him, back to its rightful place.

Discipline

The Word of God is full of examples of the discipline of meditation, especially in the Psalms. David was a man after God's own heart, and he knew God's heart by meditating and listening to Him daily. Biblical meditation is the discipline that will strengthen you, guide you, and comfort you through many treacherous seasons—especially this one. Psalm 1:2–3 (NASB) says, "But his delight is in the law of the LORD, and in His law he meditates day and night. He will be like a tree firmly planted by streams of water, which yields its fruit in its season and its leaf does not wither; and in whatever he does, he prospers." Biblical meditation takes discipline, but the Word says, "For the moment all discipline seems painful rather than pleasant; later it yields the peaceful fruit of righteousness to those who have been trained by it" (Hebrews 12:11 RSV).

I don't know about you, but I love the idea of being firmly planted (stable), by streams of water (daily refreshed), fruitful (prosperous), and last, never withering (never losing hope)! That is worth the difficult discipline of spending time with God daily!

We never want to get stuck in the belief that our religious habits and rituals redeem us. It is our personal relationship with God that redeems us—not repetitive prayers and practices. Meditation is just a discipline; it is not a religious formula. It is a tool that helps us to reach a deeper level with God, by quieting our minds and giving all our attention to Him.

Anxiety can seem like a deep hole to climb out of, but you can, and that's what you have to keep fighting for and working hard for every day. Remember that God is working on your behalf, strengthening you, refining you, and bringing you closer to deliverance. Keep working, keep pressing in, and keep going! *Don't give up! Don't quit!*

❧

APPLICATION: Take ten minutes out of your day to remember, listen, and ponder. Open your Bible and ask God what Scripture He would like you to meditate on. In prayer, ask God this one powerful question: "What is one word You have, God, to describe how You feel about me?"

Day 10

Scriptures That Heal

꧁꧂

I am a creature of a day. I am a spirit come from God, and returning to God. I want to know one thing: the way to heaven. God himself has condescended to teach me the way. He has written it down in a book. Oh, give me that book! At any price give me the book of God. Let me be a man of one book.

—JOHN WESLEY, *SERMONS ON SEVERAL OCCASIONS*

Some time ago I ventured into a very unhealthy low-fat diet. I wanted to go cold turkey off of sugar and junk food, and I needed a shove to get back into my jeans. I was eating super healthy foods and eating every two hours, but the portions were small and low calorie, and it was a drastic change from my previous eating habits. Day one was tough. I just wanted a cookie so bad! Day two, I felt physically off. And by day three, I felt my cravings subside and my appetite decrease. I was doing great and noticing some weight loss, too. My plan was to do it for only ten days and then go back to a reasonable calorie count. By day five I didn't just fall off the wagon, I parked the wagon and put a "For Sale" sign on it! Yes, I started cheating. My biggest weakness is mac and cheese. I snuck a spoonful— and by "spoonful" I mean several wooden spoons full—of the good yellowy/orangey stuff. Goose bumps went up my spine, and I literally shivered and went "Oooooooo." My body leaped!

This diet had been making me so cranky that I didn't even like to be around myself. *It can't be the diet,* I told myself in denial. I wasn't that hungry anymore, and I was craving only the blue-and-yellow box of love. I was eating balanced meals, I was getting good nutrition, but I was not eating enough. I was in starvation mode. As soon as I realized my diet crankiness was causing my husband to sleep with one eye open and my children to avoid me until after dinner, I figured I had better quit. Food affects our mood, no doubt about it.

That brings me to the next part of this story. I was going through a rough mental patch. I was beginning to gain ground in my battle with anxiety and depression, but I was still having occasional rough days. I remember feeling very anxious and depressed, and I did what I usually do to drown out my thoughts: Facebook. As I was numbly browsing, an encouraging Scripture passage came up on my feed. I remember reading it and instantly feeling goose bumps along my spine. I shivered and went "Ooooooooooo." My spirit leaped! There was a physical response to the Word of God, and I was surprised.

What was that? I asked God. He responded, *Just like your body was in starvation mode, so is your spirit.*

OUCH... That was a tough word, but God was absolutely right. The thing with physical starvation is that after a few days without food, your appetite decreases, and your body doesn't even signal that it needs food anymore, even though it is suffering. There are no more cravings and no more hunger pangs.

It's the body's way of not tormenting itself over lack of food. The same goes with spiritual starvation. Eventually we lose the craving for God and His Word, and then we have no appetite. In fact, another scary symptom of starvation is that sometimes when we have gotten our bodies into deep starvation mode, we can actually begin to detest food—even the sight of it is nauseating. Can you relate spiritually?

When we become spiritually starved, our spirits begin to deteriorate without our even being aware it's happening, but it shows up in symptoms like anger, fatigue, depression, insecurity, lack of faith, and, yes, anxiety. I am here to tell you that this is not just a *"feel good"* message. There is nothing more central to the Christian faith and our belief in Jesus Christ than knowing that He is the source of our spiritual nourishment—not Christian books (though they are great and needed), not your pastors (though they are great and needed), not your Christian radio shows or television (though they are helpful), not even MY BLOG! WHAT?! Nope, nothing will truly satisfy us but the direct Word of God.

"He humbled you and let you be hungry, and fed you with manna which you did not know, nor did your fathers know, that He might make you understand that man does not live by bread alone, but man lives by everything that proceeds out of the mouth of the LORD" (Deuteronomy 8:3 NASB). God says that without it, we go hungry, and hunger leads us to starvation, and starvation eventually leads to death. Today, we are going to perk up our appetite for the lifesaving Word of God.

Find Your Own Words

Just as our bodies can suffer physical starvation, so can our spirits. God says that He is the Bread of Life and the bread is His Word, our sustenance. However, without the Holy Spirit, the Scriptures are just words.

The Word of God lives in you. That means the Holy Spirit is working on your behalf to bring you closer to the Father. He knows your heart, your past, your failures, your future, your strengths, and your weaknesses. I don't. The Scriptures that the Lord showed me during my season in hell were for me: specific to me, breathed on by the Holy Spirit, who is working on my behalf to lead me right into the arms of my loving Father. He used the Word to walk me through past abuse, to speak to my specific fears, to break off generational curses, and to comfort me. No generic Scripture that has the words "do not fear" in it will release you. It's the *Holy Spirit* who leads you to the Word and breathes life into it. That's how Scripture heals. That is where deliverance comes from. That's where the *power* is!

You need to cling to the Word of God like it is your only meal of the day. *Study the Word as a whole and not just in part.* Do not let troubles, rain, or fear keep you away. Ask God to show you daily your manna, your word. *God, I know that all I need is in here; show me what You have for me today.* Then you search, and you keep asking, and you keep knocking, and the Word will come alive. He will show you what to read; He will show you what is for you.

I want to share with you the Scriptures listed below that healed, comforted, and delivered me in my season of torment.

I hope that God speaks to you through them as well, but my greatest wish is that you will seek the Bible for your words—words God created just for you in this season of your life.

Scriptures for Anxiety or Fear

God's love protects us.

For I am convinced that neither death nor life, neither angels nor demons, neither the present nor the future, nor any powers, neither height nor depth, nor anything else in all creation, will be able to separate us from the love of God that is in Christ Jesus our Lord. (Romans 8:38–39 NIV)

We are secure in God because He loves us.

Cast your cares on the LORD and he will sustain you; he will never let the righteous be shaken. (Psalm 55:22 NIV)

We can go to God with our worries, even the silly ones.

Do not be anxious about anything, but in every situation, by prayer and petition, with thanksgiving, present your requests to God. (Philippians 4:6 NIV)

We can trust God.

When I am afraid, I put my trust in you. (Psalm 56:3 NIV)

God is taking care of us; we are important to Him.

Therefore I tell you, do not worry about your life, what you will eat or drink; or about your body, what you will wear...Therefore do not worry about tomorrow, for tomorrow will worry about itself. Each day has enough trouble of its own. (Matthew 6:25, 34 NIV)

Only God can give us true peace.

Peace I leave with you; my peace I give you. I do not give to you as the world gives. Do not let your hearts be troubled and do not be afraid. (John 14:27 NIV)

He holds us up.

So do not fear, for I am with you; do not be dismayed, for I am your God. I will strengthen you and help you; I will uphold you with my righteous right hand. (Isaiah 41:10 NIV)

Scriptures for Depression

God gives us rest from weariness.

Come to me, all you who are weary and burdened, and I will give you rest. Take my yoke upon you and learn from me, for I am gentle and humble in heart, and you will find rest for your souls. For my yoke is easy and my burden is light. (Matthew 11:28–30 NIV)

God is ahead of us, planning out our lives.

The LORD himself goes before you and will be with you; he will never leave you nor forsake you. Do not be afraid; do not be discouraged. (Deuteronomy 31:8 NIV)

Hope leads us out of depression.

Why, my soul, are you downcast? Why so disturbed within me? Put your hope in God, for I will yet praise him, my Savior and my God. (Psalm 42:11 NIV)

God can lift up our heads to see His protection.

But you, LORD, are a shield around me, my glory, the One who lifts my head high. (Psalm 3:3 NIV)

Scriptures for Hope, Peace, and Joy

We were created for peace.

Let the peace of Christ rule in your hearts, since as members of one body you were called to peace. And be thankful. (Colossians 3:15 NIV)

We need to think on the goodness of God.

Finally, brothers and sisters, whatever is true, whatever is noble, whatever is right, whatever is pure, whatever is lovely, whatever is admirable—if anything is excellent or praiseworthy—think about such things. (Philippians 4:8 NIV)

Jesus has already gone ahead of us to secure our victory.

I have told you these things, so that in me you may have peace. In this world you will have trouble. But take heart! I have overcome the world. (John 16:33 NIV)

We can celebrate.

Go, eat your food with gladness, and drink your wine with a joyful heart, for God has already approved what you do. (Ecclesiastes 9:7 NIV)

The journey to salvation is a blessing.

Though you have not seen him, you love him; and even though you do not see him now, you believe in him and are filled with an inexpressible and glorious joy, for you are receiving the end result of your faith, the salvation of your souls. (1 Peter 1:8–9 NIV)

God fills us to overflowing!

May the God of hope fill you with all joy and peace as you trust in him, so that you may overflow with hope by the power of the Holy Spirit. (Romans 15:13 NIV)

APPLICATION: What Scriptures spoke to you? What Scriptures would you like to add to my list? Take the ones that stirred your heart and print them out. Post them on your bathroom mirror, at your desk at work, in your car, or on your emergency cue card.

Good Grief

∽⨾∾

Earth has no sorrow that heaven cannot heal.

—AUTHOR UNKNOWN

Mental illness, like depression, is complicated. It is a journey to pinpoint exactly why we are in this season. We break down for many reasons: grief, trauma, stress, brain chemistry, spiritual attacks, lack of vision and purpose, physical problems, warped thoughts, a painful past, and much more. Even strong, faith-filled people can end up spiraling into a pit of fear and despair. For me it was pretty much a combination of all the above. Years of stress, a few traumatic events, a lot of grieving, a loss of dreams, and uncontrolled thoughts all led me down this path. I even became angry with God for my disappointments. This inner turmoil in my head and heart began to break down my body and my mind, leading me straight into fear.

Our bodies, minds, and spirits are so interconnected that when one fails, the rest fail with it. "Be gracious to me, O LORD, for I am in distress; my eye is wasted from grief; my soul and my body also. For my life is spent with sorrow, and my years with sighing; my strength fails because of my iniquity, and my bones waste away" (Psalm 31:9–10 ESV). The good news is that when one part of us heals, the rest will follow.

However you got here, however deep your hole, it is no greater a task to God. He just makes a longer ladder to pull you out with. He will never leave us or forsake us, and that's a promise we have to trust God with. It is easy to trust God when we have some control, but for someone struggling with a mental breakdown, you feel nothing but a lack of control. Can we truly trust God with our whole being if we feel like we are one step closer to the loony bin, or one emotion away from losing our minds?

I have always been a little afraid of my emotions, and therefore I was never good at expressing them. They often came out in muddled sobs when I least expected or as an overwhelmed outburst. I have had hard struggles in my life, like most of us have, and I have always struggled with the fear that if I truly acknowledged my pain, I would fall into that pain so deeply that I would never climb out. "Suck it up, princess!" had been my life motto. I have always been a weather-the-storm type of person. If you had asked someone to define me, they would have responded with "Strong." I thought not showing my true feelings was strength, but in fact it was just fear.

The pain of all my abandonment and failures was too deep, and way too painful to go near, so I kept it hidden under the facade of "It's in the past, and God has redeemed me. Amen?!" It's not that I walked around as a fake person. I was able to talk about my past. However, I had never been able to discuss the pain of it with others or myself. *All fear!*

Then one night, during my months of burnout before my breakdown, I had a dream. God speaks to me often in dreams, probably because I never leave room for a commercial break in my mind during the day. In this particular dream, I was in the gym of a busy high school and two paramedics raced in. I was wondering why they were there, when suddenly they locked eyes with me and came toward me. "You need to come with us, ma'am," they said sternly. "You're in serious heart failure." They took me out into the hallway and began assessing me and working on me. All the while I was thinking, *I'm fine!* But they insisted I was at great risk.

I was rattled by the dream. I couldn't get it off my mind. I now know that God was trying to warn me of something—He was telling me that my heart was sick, and I needed restoration. I broke down only a few months later. My heart was very sick, and I needed some deep heart healing. This shocked me, because I thought I was strong, since I didn't feel pain or live in the past. But the hard question was, if I never dealt with the pain, where did the pain go? It doesn't evaporate on a sunny day. It sits stagnated in the subconscious, waiting to blow. How silly of me to think that I could bury it and try to forget it. Then God taught me how to grieve.

Grief is not an emotion set aside only for death. Grief can accompany a loss of any kind: loss of a marriage, a child's rebellion, loss of innocence, destruction of your past, loss of your health, knowing what you should never have known as a child, or the failure of your dreams. We are lousy at grief, especially in North America, where our motto is: "Emotions are bad—show no pain." This is a destructive way to live. When garbage comes in, it has to get out. We can release it in a healthy way, or it will leak out or burst out in the form of anger, anxiety, dependency, addiction, you name it. It will surface eventually. We

live our day-to-day lives shoving down our pain and are completely oblivious to the fact that it is leaking toxicity throughout our minds and, yes, even our physical bodies. Not until it is
brought into consciousness, to the front of our minds, and dealt
with can we stop its toxic reign. So what I am saying is this:
Deal with your stuff before it deals with you!

Why We Need to Grieve

When we draw near to Him, He draws near to us. The
healthy way to handle the brokenness that has entered
our lives is through the uninhibited grief that we lay
before God. Grief is as necessary to the soul's health
as joy is. When we draw near to God with our sorrow,
He draws near to us, holds our crushed spirit in His
hands, and saves us. "The LORD is near to the brokenhearted and saves the crushed in spirit" (Psalm 34:18
ESV).

God has set aside seasons for grief. The other reason we
are to grieve before God is because God says that there
is a time set aside in our lives for sorrow. It is the circle
of life, necessary for the following seasons. Just like fall
is to winter, and winter is to spring.

For everything there is a season, and a time for every matter under heaven: a time to be born, and a time to die; a

time to plant, and a time to pluck up what is planted; a time to kill, and a time to heal; a time to break down, and a time to build up; a time to weep, and a time to laugh; a time to mourn, and a time to dance; a time to cast away stones, and a time to gather stones together; a time to embrace, and a time to refrain from embracing.

ECCLESIASTES 3:1–5 ESV

Grieving allows God to comfort us. When we mourn before God, and expose to Him the depths of our hearts, He comforts us and calls us His children. "Seeing the crowds, he went up on the mountain, and when he sat down, his disciples came to him. And he opened his mouth and taught them, saying: 'Blessed are the poor in spirit, for theirs is the kingdom of heaven. Blessed are those who mourn, for they shall be comforted'" (Matthew 5:1–4 ESV).

When I felt like the ground was about to crumble beneath my feet, God started telling me to come and grieve before Him. I resisted at first, afraid of the pain, because every day was an intense mental and emotional battle. To be honest, my pride kept telling me I didn't need it. But soon God started peeling away the walls without my permission. The grief started coming, whether I wanted it to or not. I was left with the most immense raw pain, and it increased daily. What was happening?

I bargained with God not to take me there. But He had heard my cry for freedom from fear and wasn't relenting until He answered it fully, despite my resistance. Once you phone 911, you can't *un*phone the emergency center. God isn't just a symptom healer. He is *The Healer*. So as the pain surfaced like never before, I thought I would die in it. Then one day I became undone. I fell to my knees, literally, and I grieved and I grieved and I grieved before the Lord. I grieved through my past, my abandonment, my abuses, my failures, my mistakes, and my sins. I grieved so hard that I was physically exhausted, unable to move. Then something amazing happened.

I began to feel the overwhelming peace and the love of God consume me. I could barely sit upright. He downloaded supernatural healing into me, and I received every ounce of it. He walked me through forgiveness, and He began to show me glimmers of promise for my future, some that I am living out right now! I sat completely engulfed in God's presence and hope. That was a major turning point for my life and my mental health. I went to Him brokenhearted—with a crushed spirit. It almost wore me out physically to do it, but He drew near and He saved me. *Grieving* in the presence of God—as a verb, an action before God—is as powerful as any form of therapy. I have learned now to go to God with my deep anger and hurts immediately. I can just be me—even an irrational version of me—and I know that when I have laid it before Him, in complete honesty and grief, He will comfort me and restore my soul. This is where the deep work is done.

APPLICATION: Sometimes we need help to grieve. Who can you go to professionally or personally to ask for help? What major events in your life do you need to grieve? Write them down and keep them close as you spend time with God. Ask God to help you.

Day 12

Healing the Past

∾

He heals the brokenhearted and binds up their wounds.

—Psalm 147:3 ESV

Before we begin today's focus, I want to encourage you with this truth: A person living with anxiety can be seen as weak, but I want to tell you that people living with anxiety are some of the most courageous people I know. The fact that you get up every day and keep going, keep working, and keep loving those around you is a sign of immense courage. You have to fight and face your fears *every day*. The fact that you are fighting through them, and facing them despite your trembling, shows a great strength within you. Keep going! Don't give up hope! When David was being told he didn't have it in him to fight Goliath, he responded:

Your servant has been keeping his father's sheep. When a lion or a bear came and carried off a sheep from the flock, I went after it, struck it and rescued the sheep from its mouth. When it turned on me, I seized it by its hair, struck it and killed it. Your servant has killed both the lion and the bear; this uncircumcised Philistine will be like one of them, because he has defied the armies of the living God.

1 Samuel 17:34–36 NIV

I know in your lifetime you have been strong, and you have had to fight some lions. You have probably had to fight the bears! But know this: *You can also fight the giant!*

We all make giant mistakes. Every single one of us who has ever breathed a breath on this earth has fallen short of God's glory. We all experience hurts; we are born into a world of very broken people, and it is impossible to get through life without some injury to our hearts and souls. Today, I want you to begin the process of healing life's hurts so that you can get back up on your feet and start living your life with wholeness, free from fear and free from bondage.

Professional Counseling

For the majority of us struggling with anxiety and panic, even depression, too, this will not be something we can do on our own. Trying to heal your own pain is like trying to repair your own car engine. Sometimes we become used to the stalling, the leaks, and the strange engine noises—we think it's normal, because the car is still running. A professional knows what to look for and how to find the root of the issue. For the majority of us, myself included, we need a professional therapist to help us through this process of healing the past. Here are a few tips on finding a good therapist:

Find someone who respects your faith. If you are a Christian, there are a lot of Christian counseling centers out there, but Christian counseling is not necessary.

As long as there is freedom to express your faith and your healing journey with God's hand in it, then that is good therapy.

You should feel better within the first three visits. It is a process, and it can take months or years or only a few sessions to begin the healing process, but either way you should begin to feel like you are heading in an upward direction by the third or fourth visit.

Be transparent. If you hold back the truth and depth of your torments and pain, you will not receive the healing you need. You need to be as transparent as possible and share openly your disappointments, failures, grievances, hurts, and offenses.

Don't become dependent. A good therapist's job is to get you out of their office as soon as possible. Chances are, when they begin to break up with you, you won't feel ready. Know that weaning you from therapy is all part of your recovery, and it is a good sign that your therapist thinks you are ready to start taking your life back!

Repentance before God

I can't say I like the word "repentance" very much, because it has been misused to hurt people rather than to help people. But within the context of God's love for us, this is a necessary part of our journey. Repentance isn't about feeling guilty for what we have done, but rather about acknowledging that the mistakes we made in the past pushed us away from God, and we are making a conscious choice to make a change back toward God.

Our failures and big messes in our lives can cause great anxiety in the future for many reasons. We may be afraid of getting caught or of the past coming back to haunt us. We might fear being out of control again or facing the consequences of those actions. We might also be fearful of punishment (from God or man) for our mistakes. These fears can create a very strong case for anxiety to reign in our lives. We don't deserve to be happy and feel peace after all that we have done, do we? Well, the truth is, when we repent and reconcile to God, He sees us as unblemished and calls us His children. It's as simple as acknowledging our sins before God and accepting His forgiveness.

Forgiveness

I mentioned God stirring up immense pain that grew and grew until I laid it down before Him. Part of that process was having to forgive others for their offenses toward me. I won't go into great detail, but I have experienced a lot of pain with regard to men in my life. It is not easy to write about my past, not because it brings pain—God has healed that—but because I have come so far in healing from my past that it seems like I am writing about a girl I once knew. I have worked through a lot of my past as I have journeyed closer to God. But as it all came to a head in anxiety, I realized, quite traumatically, that this pain was much deeper than I had thought. I was in severe heart failure!

As God kept bringing up this pain as fresh as it had been years prior, He brought me through forgiveness. The image God showed me as I prayed forever changed the way I looked at forgiveness. As I prayed and as the memories welled up inside of me—all the rejection, the pain, the shame, the abandonment, the defilement—I saw a vision of every man who had hurt me standing in an execution-style row, all bound, gagged, and clothed in prison garb, all waiting for the call to be executed. Jesus was present and standing beside me as I faced the first man in the line of fire. Jesus turned to me and said, *Just say when.* God had given me all authority to have them executed. I, with my unforgiveness, had been given total authority to decide these men's fate.

I wrestled hard in that moment. I knew it wasn't my right to decide their fate, but I knew that my unforgiveness was putting me in a position to judge. In that moment I turned to Jesus and said painfully, *I release them to You.* It was extremely difficult to face each one and *let him go.* One by one, I released the prisoners (the ones I held captive to my unforgiveness), and one by one I released the authority back to God. Their judgment was no longer mine, but, rightfully, God's. By letting them go, I let the pain go, too.

I share that with you to show you the power of unforgiveness, how it opposes God's authority in our lives and keeps the victim and us captive. This was a deep root issue in my life, and I had to dig pretty far to find it. But when God brought it to the surface, I allowed Him the freedom to work in my mind. As we begin to heal life's hurts, we will begin to see the roots of anxiety die.

Finding the Lies

Do you ever find that the simplest of prayers sometimes hold immense power? If it hadn't been for one simple prayer I prayed one day, I would not have been set free. A few months before my nervous breakdown I prayed, *God, reveal to me the greatest lie in my life.* Wow, dangerous prayer! Tormenting fear is always rooted in a lie, as are the pain and unforgiveness we carry in our hearts. Exposing the lie exposes the truth, and the truth sets us free. The biggest lie I believed was that God didn't love me. "Praise the LORD. How good it is to sing praises to our God, how pleasant and fitting to praise him! The LORD builds up Jerusalem; he gathers the exiles of Israel. He heals the brokenhearted and binds up their wounds" (Psalm 147:1–3 NIV).

⊱⊰

APPLICATION: Take a huge step of courage today and ask God to show you the biggest lie you believe. When God reveals it to you, begin to pray through that lie and study the truth.

Day 13

Taking Your Thoughts Captive

❧

With a new day comes new strength and new thoughts.
—ELEANOR ROOSEVELT, "MY DAY," JANUARY 8, 1936

Did you know that the fearful thoughts in your head have actually formed physical structures in your brain? It has been proven by science that your thoughts can actually affect your body's DNA and rewire the brain. Dr. Caroline Leaf, a Christian neuroscientist, says that 75 to 98 percent of all illnesses[1]— mental, physical, and emotional—begin from our thoughts. This is a terrifying thought, because how many years have we spent in negative, anxious thinking?

This is living proof that our bodies, minds, and spirits are interconnected and affecting one another all the time, sometimes in a very serious way. In Proverbs, Solomon stated, "A cheerful heart is good medicine, but a crushed spirit dries up the bones" (17:22 NIV). Even God warns us that our state of mind and emotions affect our health. The good news here, though, is that the effect is not permanent, and we actually have the ability to rewire our brains and change our DNA by changing our thinking.

God has gifted each of us with a creative mind, but like any gift, if it is not grounded in Christ it can begin to rob us of our joy and peace. My creative mind loves to tell stories and create scenarios. I can never just drive over a bridge and look at the view, because every time I do, I picture myself driving off and plummeting to the ground in a fiery crash. If my husband is four minutes late from work, I've already decided how I'll react when the police show up at my door. My mind has a very big imagination. It can be *amazing* and it can be *tormenting*. I am thankful for my creative mind, but if my negative and uncontrolled thoughts are robbing me of my peace, then I need to learn how to control them.

There is a lot of instruction in the Bible about controlling our thoughts. Jesus said that the Father judges our thoughts even before our actions reveal them. We think that these harmful and anxious thoughts are uncontrollable, but that is exactly what Satan would have us believe to ensure we stay overwhelmed by them. We may not be able to control what thoughts knock on the door of our minds, but we have total control over which ones we let in. Throughout the Word of God, God is insistently trying to teach us how to guard our thoughts, because He knows that this is the Achilles' heel of our soul and salvation.

God said we are to make sure our thoughts are disciplined and do not exalt themselves against the promises and truth of God. "We demolish arguments and every pretension that sets itself up against the knowledge of God, and we take captive every thought to make it obedient to Christ" (2 Corinthians 10:5 NIV).

My thoughts were irrational, overdramatic, and out of control. They were constant, unwelcome, and completely terrifying. They had the power to throw me into the fetal position for hours. Thoughts like *Was that mole on my face there before? What if it's cancer?* or *I just forgot it was Sunday. Am I going crazy?* or *My throat feels tight. What if it's an allergic reaction and my throat closes up and I die?*

As chaotic and unpredictable as my thoughts were, when I began to apply the biblical principle of taking my thoughts captive, I began to see major breakthroughs. And soon each tormenting thought loosened its grip on me, until eventually they stopped coming around.

I had a dream one night where I climbed into the attic of my house. Little destructive creatures were given free rein in the attic, and they were climbing over all the storage boxes and rummaging through all my belongings. In the corner was a jail cell, and Jesus was locked away in that cell. Then the Lord spoke to me: *Sarah, you need to release Me into your mind and give Me full access.* I know my dreams are bizarre, but how else could God speak to me, when during the day Satan had my full attention? I realized that there was a battle going on in my mind, and I needed to begin releasing the Word of God and take control back.

Though that was a very spiritual dream, we do not have to overspiritualize taking our thoughts captive. Paul's instructions for this can be more practical than spiritually figurative. I think that some thoughts come straight from the pit of hell, and others are simply our overwhelmed minds trying to protect us. We will get into the spiritual warfare side of things in the next chapter, but for today we will learn how to practically take our thoughts captive, judge the thoughts that come, and make them obedient.

How to Take Your Thoughts Captive

Dump the what-ifs. Every anxious thought is usually preceded by a what-if statement.

- What if they are late because they were in a car accident?

- What if I fail the exam and I have to repeat school?

- What if they reject me and I don't get the job?

- What if I touched something that has a germ on it that will make me sick?

- What if I eat that piece of shrimp and choke?

- What if I'm like this forever and I destroy my whole life?

- What if I have a panic attack and faint in the middle of the meeting?

     When the what-ifs come, this is when we take the thought captive. Take time to stop and look back and ask yourself, *What was the what-if statement that set me off?* It's difficult trying to sort through all the other thoughts that flood in afterward, so finding the source of the anxiety— *the initial thought*—will help you be able to face it with truth.

Consider cognitive behavioral therapy (CBT). This is groundbreaking therapy that is very successful in treating anxiety and depression. Yet it is the least common form of therapy available. CBT teaches you how to take your thoughts captive. It helps you to recognize warped thoughts, separate them from healthy ones, and to speak truth back to the lie. One thing I learned through understanding cognitive behavioral therapy was how to tackle those insistent what-if thoughts. Let me give you an example of how to deal with a what-if thought:

1. Acknowledge the what-if.

2. Answer the what-if with a word of extreme hope. For example, you might think, *What if I fail this test?* Answer that thought with, *What if I pass and make the honor roll?*

3. Answer the what-if with humor. For example, if you were to think, *What if I get so depressed that I become suicidal?* answer that with, *What if I get so happy that I am annoying to be around?* Or, *What if my husband is late because he is dead and I am a widow and have to raise five kids alone?* Answer: *What if he comes home with flowers, a box of chocolates, and a maid, and I am so thrilled that we end up with baby number six?*

   You may have chuckled reading the actual responses I gave myself, and that's the point. When we stop taking ourselves so seriously and make light of our anxiety, it eases the intensity of the thoughts. You ask me a ridiculous question; I'm going to give you a ridiculous response.

I have *always* been a what-if person. Even before my breakdown, I always had underlying anxiety like this, but when I learned to take my thoughts captive, I actually renewed my mind to the point where I don't think that way anymore. God has actually reprogrammed my mind for peace.

Rebuke the thought. I don't even want to know what people thought of me during that time when I would burst out with a strong "No!" or "That's a lie!" or "No more!" Paul says we are to take our thoughts captive. This means to recognize a wrong thought and interrogate it. We say a strong "No!" to the lies that exalt themselves against God's promises. Don't worry what others think. You need to take control and discipline your mind. A passive *Well, that wasn't very nice* to yourself isn't going to intimidate the thought that just told you, *You're probably going to die of cancer just like your mom did.*

Fill your head with good. When we are in the thick of battle we do not all of a sudden transform into She-Ra (Princess of Power) or the Hulk. What I am trying to say is that the battle isn't won by the strength we have during the fight, but the strength we had going into it. God says *He strengthens us for battle!* It is in between the times of mental assault that the battle will be won, and this Scripture tells us exactly how: "Finally, brothers and sisters, whatever is true, whatever is noble, whatever is right, whatever is pure, whatever is lovely, whatever is admirable—if anything is excellent or praiseworthy—think about such things" (Philippians 4:8 NIV).

This truth is the biggest weapon you will use to literally change the physical structure of your mind. Your warped thoughts will not stand in your mind against a brain that is marinated in good things. When you combat negative thoughts with the Word of God and with other good things, the chemicals released from the positive thoughts will literally melt away the negative structures in your brain. The mind can begin to renew itself in as little as twenty-one days.[2]

This is where Christians become resistant, because some have spread much fear about certain methods of meditation or relaxation techniques—mindfulness, for example. Mindfulness was derived from Buddhist meditation. It is the act of bringing all your attention into the present moment and being accepting of all your sensations, emotions, and surroundings. Other forms of mindful thinking are used to imagine a peaceful place, trying to feel, smell, and hear it with your mind. I do agree that we need to be very cautious to examine each form of meditation that we are considering, as I mentioned earlier. However, my advice is that we all just need to calm down! Closing your eyes and imagining a beautiful, sunny field with butterflies and harp music is not going to ensnare you, because it is biblical!

Remember, God created it all. Satan did not create *mindful thinking* for the New Age Movement. He stole it from God and twisted it! Paul did not say whatever is religious, whatever is only Christian, whatever is approved by your pastor, meditate on these things. He said, "Whatever is true, whatever is noble, whatever is right, whatever is pure, whatever is lovely, whatever is admirable—if anything is excellent or praiseworthy— think about such things" (Philippians 4:8 NIV). God created the field and the butterflies and the harp music, and choosing to move your thoughts from suicide to God's creation is as biblical as it gets.

Use your imagination throughout the day to create, to think of good things, to dwell on lovely things. Watch comedies, turn off the news, avoid toxic people, and surround yourself with beauty, encouragement, uplifting music, and the Word of God. Listen to the Word, sing, dance, laugh. Close your eyes and imagine yourself free and running through fields of poppies. Do what you can all day long to fill your mind with good.

❦

APPLICATION: Think of your last fearful thought. How could you have responded differently to that thought? Write out the last major what-if thought. Did it come true? Write out a new positive what-if statement.

Day 14

Spiritual Deliverance

⚜

Is anyone crying for help? GOD is listening, ready to rescue you.

—PSALM 34:17 MSG

Over the past thirteen days we have talked about our physical health, our relationship with God, our thoughts, and practical ways to deal with panic and anxiety. Your running shoes are on, your pantry is full of whole foods, your Bible is by your bedside and worn, and your thoughts are getting a licking, but all that won't change the fact that you still have a wolf gnawing at your ankles trying to devour you.

If Satan can take a strong man or woman such as yourself and get you consumed with terror and physical breakdown, questioning God's faithfulness, then he has just disarmed another child of God. You are in for a battle. Your life depends on it. I don't say that to alarm you, or to add more fear, but I think you are already aware of how debilitating this is and how defeated you feel. We need to be fully aware that we are not in a battle just against our own flesh but one against principalities and powers (see Ephesians 6:12). As long as the terrorist of your soul can keep you crippled in fear, the plans and purposes that God has for you will be thwarted.

I want to remind you of the truth that Satan has no authority over your body or your life; he just intimidates you to think
he does. He has stolen what belongs to the Lord; he has robbed
you of your inheritance (which is peace and joy). He turns your
worship from God toward him. He thinks he is winning. You
may even think he is winning. How do you feel about this? Does
it make you mad? *I hope so!* Mad enough to fight back? *I hope so!*

You have probably learned by now that I am a dreamer,
probably because my mind never. Stops. Ever. One night God
spoke to me very clearly about the battle I was in. In my dream,
the King appeared with armies behind Him and a procession
of musicians and soldiers. I knelt down and the King came over
to me and said, *You're in for a fight, Sarah. It's a hard fight, but you
are guaranteed victory.* Then He dashed off to war, and I followed
quickly, panicked that I might lose sight of where the King was
leading me.

We are guaranteed victory, and when we choose to go into
a battle knowing we will win and the enemy will be defeated,
we fight harder. How would you fight in a battle that you were
guaranteed to win?

God says that we are *more than conquerors!* This means that
you're not only going to win this battle, you are going to gain
from it. You are going to come out of this with more than you
went in with! This is a powerful truth in my life now. Mind-sets
and issues I carried with me for years fell off of me as I sought
freedom from anxiety.

Nothing is going to separate you from the love that God has
for you, the plans and blessings He has for you—not even your

mind or your harmful thoughts or your weird imaginings or your irrational fears! *You are already free!*

> What then shall we say to these things? If God is for us, who is against us? He who did not spare His own Son, but delivered Him over for us all, how will He not also with Him freely give us all things? Who will bring a charge against God's elect? God is the one who justifies; who is the one who condemns? Christ Jesus is He who died, yes, rather who was raised, who is at the right hand of God, who also intercedes for us. Who will separate us from the love of Christ? Will tribulation, or distress, or persecution, or famine, or nakedness, or peril, or sword?
>
> ROMANS 8:31–35 NASB

My friends, Satan has you deceived. He is whispering in your ear that you are perishing, and I am here to tell you, as a victorious survivor of the battle, that is a lie. Now is the time to gird yourself with the truth and lift up your sword. You are going to battle!

How Does God Respond to Our Captivity?

I don't blame you for having a shaky faith at this time. Your foundation has been ripped out from under you. Often when we are in a mental health crisis, we are in a spiritual crisis, too. One of the lies we may believe is that God is watching our suffering from a cloud, patiently trying to teach us something.

We're going to prove this lie false by opening up the Word of God, which is alive and active and sharper than a double-edged sword! This Scripture is going to lead us to understand how God responds to our captivity.

Psalm 18:1–19, 28–39, 46, 50 (NKJV)

DAVID CRIES OUT TO GOD

I will love You, O LORD, my strength.
The LORD is my rock and my fortress and my deliverer;
My God, my strength, in whom I will trust;
My shield and the horn of my salvation, my stronghold.
I will call upon the LORD, who is worthy to be praised;
So shall I be saved from my enemies.

The pangs of death surrounded me,
And the floods of ungodliness made me afraid.
The sorrows of Sheol surrounded me;
The snares of death confronted me.
In my distress I called upon the LORD,
And cried out to my God;

GOD'S RESPONSE

He heard my voice from His temple,
And my cry came before Him, even to His ears.

Then the earth shook and trembled;
The foundations of the hills also quaked and were shaken,
Because He was angry.

Smoke went up from His nostrils,
And devouring fire from His mouth;
Coals were kindled by it.
He bowed the heavens also, and came down
With darkness under His feet.
And He rode upon a cherub, and flew;
He flew upon the wings of the wind.
He made darkness His secret place;
His canopy around Him was dark waters
And thick clouds of the skies.
From the brightness before Him,
His thick clouds passed with hailstones and coals of fire.

The Lord *thundered from heaven,*
And the Most High uttered His voice,
Hailstones and coals of fire.
He sent out His arrows and scattered the foe,
Lightnings in abundance, and He vanquished them.
Then the channels of the sea were seen,
The foundations of the world were uncovered
At Your rebuke, O Lord,
At the blast of the breath of Your nostrils.

He sent from above, He took me;
He drew me out of many waters.
He delivered me from my strong enemy,
From those who hated me,
For they were too strong for me.

They confronted me in the day of my calamity,
But the Lord *was my support.*
He also brought me out into a broad place;
He delivered me because He delighted in me . . .

AND THEN DAVID RESPONDS

For You will light my lamp;
The Lord *my God will enlighten my darkness.*
For by You I can run against a troop,
By my God I can leap over a wall.
As for God, His way is perfect;
The word of the Lord *is proven;*
He is a shield to all who trust in Him.

For who is God, except the Lord*?*
And who is a rock, except our God?
It is God who arms me with strength,
And makes my way perfect.
He makes my feet like the feet of deer,
And sets me on my high places.
He teaches my hands to make war,
So that my arms can bend a bow of bronze.

You have also given me the shield of Your salvation;
Your right hand has held me up,
Your gentleness has made me great.
You enlarged my path under me,
So my feet did not slip.

I have pursued my enemies and overtaken them;
Neither did I turn back again till they were destroyed.
I have wounded them,
So that they could not rise;
They have fallen under my feet.
For You have armed me with strength for the battle . . .

The LORD *lives!*
Blessed be my Rock!
Let the God of my salvation be exalted . . .

Great deliverance He gives to His king,
And shows mercy to His anointed.

This Scripture has been the center of my life for more than a year. God's words have way more power in them than mine ever will. When I read this, I was at the point of giving up, ready to accept my fear and anxiety and learn to live with the torment of fear. I felt completely defeated. I used to believe the lie that God was a passive God who relishes in our plight because we deserve it, but when I began to read His Word and believe it, I began to realize that God is a passionate, loving Father who gets angered by our captivity and will do anything to set us free.

The Lord wants you free. He is angered by your captivity. He's not angry at *you*, but at the enemy who has ensnared you. God has heard your cries for deliverance and He is coming, He is fuming, and He is enraging the heavens on your behalf. God, right now, even as you are reading this, is strengthening *your* hands for battle. He is equipping *you* to stand against your enemies. He is teaching *you* to fight, so that *you* will indeed be able to leap over the next wall that comes your way, so that *you* will become more than a conqueror!

What Is Deliverance?

When I use the word "deliverance," many people assume or picture in their minds a demonic thrashing with priests sprinkling holy water. Eek! If that were always true, then we would probably avoid asking God for deliverance. Though this is absolutely necessary for some, you should seek mature spiritual counseling if you feel such a manifestation may occur. Just remember that Satan is under our feet, thanks to Jesus' authority (see Matthew 8:28–34).

For today, I am not necessarily talking about this dramatic display of deliverance.

Deliverance simply means "the state of being saved from something dangerous or unpleasant." Deliverance is a supernatural breaking off of Satan's hold on us, his dominion over our minds, our souls, and even our bodies, just like when God delivered the Israelites out of Egypt, Daniel from the lion's den, and David from his enemies. Deliverance is a supernatural victory that leaves us with more than we lost in the first place.

How to Receive Deliverance

Your prayers—"In my distress I called to the LORD; I cried to my God for help" (Psalm 18:6 NIV). David cried out to God for his deliverance. When we cry out to God, He hears us. Our prayers are effective, and we need to ask God for our deliverance.

The prayers of others—You need the army of God. You need the saints. You need people praying for you! You will not get through this alone. Call in the troops. Don't be ashamed. Don't let the enemy use your fear of man to keep you from your deliverance.

Desperation before reputation—How badly do you want to be free? Personally, I was tremendously desperate. I was a fool before the Lord and others. I didn't care. I was desperate for healing. I would attend my regular Bible study, and I was that crazy lady on her knees crying aloud during worship. I was that person who always went up for prayer. I was unhindered before God. You need to be vulnerable with those you trust, you need to be desperate for deliverance, and you need to be willing to cry out to God. "The LORD is near to all who call on him, to all who call on him *in truth*. He fulfills the desires of those who fear him; he hears their cry and saves them. The LORD watches over all who love him, but all the wicked he will destroy" (Psalm 145:18–20 NIV; emphasis mine).

Fasting—In the beginning I was too weak to fast, so I would ask my husband to fast for me. Every time he fasted for me, I would receive a breakthrough. When I was stronger, I fasted, and it was always effective.

Professor and author Bill Thrasher says, "The abstinence is not to be an end in itself but rather for the purpose of being separated to the Lord and to concentrate on godliness. This kind of fasting reduces the influence of our own self-will and invites the Holy Spirit to do a more intense work in us."[1]

The Word of God—We talked about how powerful words and Scriptures are. The Word of God is more than just powerful; it is a flat-out assault on the enemy. It is spiritual warfare! The more you continue to declare and read aloud the Word of God and His promises, the more ground you are taking in your mind and in your soul.

Perspective—It's okay to be angry with God (if that's where you are at). He wants us to come to Him in truth. Remember, though, that God is not only fighting on your behalf, but He is also strengthening you for the battle. God wants to teach you how to *leap* over this wall, so He doesn't have to rescue you out of this again. God is trying to teach you how to handle His sword. He's trying to strengthen you, and He's trying to lead you out in such a way that you will never return to your bondage! "When Pharaoh let the people go, God did not lead them by way of the land of the Philistines, although that was near. For God said, 'Lest the people change their minds when they see war and return to Egypt'" (Exodus 13:17 ESV).

Praise God for the victories—Every inch is a victory, whether big or small. We must be in an attitude of praise and thankfulness to God for the steps we are taking. When we focus on how far we have to go instead of how far we have come, we can easily be discouraged. Look how far you have come, praise God for the ground you just conquered, and rejoice in it!

Know you have already won!—The truth is, God has already won the battle. "But thanks be to God, who gives us the victory through our Lord Jesus Christ. Therefore, my beloved brethren, be steadfast, immovable, always abounding in the work of the Lord, knowing that your toil is not in vain in the Lord" (1 Corinthians 15:57–58 NASB).

❧

APPLICATION: Journal today how you feel knowing that God desires for you to be set free. How does it feel knowing that He is angered not at you, but at your bondage? How has this Scripture changed how you perceive God? Are you ready to accept His freedom?

Day 15

For Your Loved Ones

What does love look like? It has the hands to help others. It has the feet to hasten to the poor and needy. It has eyes to see misery and want. It has the ears to hear the sighs and sorrows of men. That is what love looks like.

—St. Augustine

This chapter is for your loved ones, the ones who are doing their best, with the knowledge they have, to help you through this. So go ahead and pass this chapter on to them...

I recently asked my husband if it was hard for him to see me in pain when I was in labor with our babies—especially the one that weighed in at ten and a half pounds at birth. His response was, "Yes, but not as hard as watching you go through anxiety and panic."

I am sure that you are just as taken aback by what is happening to your loved one as the person you love is. It can be confusing, discouraging, and fearful for all involved. It puts strain on families, marriages, and friendships. I want to help you help your loved one with some understanding and some wisdom for you. I want to help you to know when to push and when to support, when to be assertive and when to be compassionate.

I want to give you some practical advice on how to help your loved one not only cope with anxiety but overcome it.

If your loved one is reading this book and passing this chapter on to you, then he or she is a fighter and doesn't want to be anxious forever. And if you're reading this willingly, then you don't want your loved one to be fearful forever, either. Let's conclude, then, that you are reading this because you desire with your whole heart to link arms with your loved one and see that person through this to complete healing, not just symptom management.

Anxiety, panic, and even depression are complex illnesses. It's important for you to understand, as part of the support system, that anxiety is not just a breakdown of the mind. It is a physical, mental, and spiritual breakdown. In order for your loved one to truly recover, all three elements of the person need care. Your loved one needs physical rest, nutrition, and exercise. They need spiritual support, prayer, fasting, and the Word of God. They need the mental strength gained through learning how to control their thoughts, therapy, and perhaps medication.

In this book, I have been covering all aspects of recovery: body, mind, and spirit. It would be good for you to read through some of the things I have been teaching in order to better help and guide your loved one. But in this chapter I am going to give you some tips.

The Best Way You Can Help

Defend their rest. Your loved one's mind is overwhelmed, their body is breaking down, and their spirit is weary.

Your loved one is in need of rest—physical rest, mental rest, and spiritual rest. If you are a spouse, give them times every day to rest in quiet. (Give them verbal permission!)

Pastors, release them, guilt-free, from duties until they are well again. Let them just come and rest in God's presence. (Give them verbal permission!)

Friends, keep your friend accountable about not taking on too much. Empower them to say *no* to things. Let them be vulnerable. (Give them verbal permission!)

Listen well. Don't try to offer suggestions on how they should feel or what they can do to not feel. The truth is they feel, and they don't want to, and if they could do something about it, they would. Listening is not a passive part to play. It is a powerful outlet for someone caught in their thoughts. Sometimes fears are so irrational that the person battling them keeps them inside because they are too afraid of your response. They know the fear is bizarre and unfounded, but just speaking them out loud can break the fears instantly.

Use prompting questions to help your loved one talk.

- What are your recent fears?

- How are you coping?

- Can I do anything to help you rest?

- Are there any anxious thoughts you want to share?

People suffering with anxiety and panic often feel ashamed about how they think and feel. They want to share their inner darkness, but it's too risky to share for fear of being judged or having others overreact. They need to be asked in order to draw them out. Help your loved one to live outside their head and expose their truth. It is powerful, and they need you. Don't just ask them, "How are you?" Ask them, in private, "How has your anxiety been? Are you sleeping well? Are you getting enough support?" Be specific about what you ask them, and then listen.

Help them make a plan and find help. More than ever your loved one needs your support and your love, but you cannot rescue them from this alone. Depending on the severity of their anxiety, they may need to see their family doctor. They may need professional counseling or medication. Be as involved in their professional help as you can be.

Don't pressure them to get better. "I miss the old you" is a common complaint of a loved one to their suffering spouse. This can be perceived as a very insensitive comment, because they miss the old them, too, and it can weigh them down with a lot of unnecessary guilt. The encouraging news is that when your loved one gets through this dark season, they will be stronger for it. They become a person who now has boundaries, who makes their health a priority, and who can handle stressful situations better. Grow with them, change with them. It's healthy to push them, but it is unproductive to guilt them or pressure them into recovery.

Be patient. Be patient when they can't watch the news anymore, or they sleep a lot more. Be patient if they aren't ready to host a house party or serve in church. Be patient with their recovery. It takes time. Part of learning to recover from an anxiety breakdown is learning to voice what you can or cannot handle.

Know when they are stuck. A sure warning sign that they are stuck is that they have accepted it as "just the way they are," or they start making major life changes to avoid triggers. Avoiding public places or using unhealthy coping mechanisms—drugs, alcohol, excessive television—are all signs of an anxiety sufferer stuck in their fears.

Push when they are stuck. This is when you push to say, "What do we need to do to move to the next level in your recovery?"

Don't enable phobias. If they are starting to exhibit specific phobias like fear of heights, certain foods, or animals, don't throw it in their face and force them into a situation where they have to face it head-on, but don't enable their fears, either, by accommodating them. You are only enabling and reinforcing the fears if you are adjusting your behaviors and experiences to their fears. Get them professional help if the fear becomes debilitating.

Seek God aggressively on their behalf. They need your prayers—not just passive prayers, they need you warring for them. Don't ever stop.

Listen to God on their behalf. I was struggling with sleep; it was a torment to me. One day my pastor phoned and had an encouraging Scripture for me. It was exactly what I needed to hear, and it broke the curse of sleep over me. She was praying for me and listening to God for me. My husband would often say, "I was praying, and I just feel certain that this won't be forever, that God is allowing this for a reason, and you're going to get through this, and it's coming soon." He was warring on my behalf and listening on my behalf, and his encouragement was an anchor for me.

Keep them accountable. Are they resting? Are they being spiritually fed? Are they taking their medication? Are they exercising? Don't be afraid to be assertive in helping them do what they need to do to heal.

Join them in recovery. I just mentioned the importance of spending time with God, resting, and exercising. Not a bad idea for you, too, eh? Join your loved one in their recovery. Walk with them daily, study the Bible together, and take care of your own mental health.

Have fun! Be creative. What fun things can you do to help them distract their mind?

Laugh together. Laughter is great medicine; find ways to laugh together.

Know it's only for a season. You and your loved one may feel like this will last forever, but it won't.

Take care of yourself. The last thing your loved one needs is you in the same boat. Put on your oxygen mask before assisting others. Take time for yourself, and build yourself up.

Love them. Love is powerful. Love is one of the most powerful tools against fear. In fact, the Bible says that love casts out all fear! Love your loved one where they are. Show them and tell them as often as you can.

How to Help Someone through a Panic Attack

- Give them room. They may want to change locations. Go with them.

- Don't try to talk them out of it. Just be present and tell them calmly it's going to be okay. (Don't talk too much.)

- Remind them to breathe.

- Tell them they are not dying. Be firm but kind.

- Don't tell them that they have nothing to fear or that they are being irrational. (Do tell them they will get past this.)

- Help them relax and get comfortable as they are calming down.

- Hug them afterward and reassure them. (They will be feeling embarrassed.)

Back to you—I hope this helps your loved ones to better understand how to help you, but the best way for you to get the help you need, the way you need it, is to communicate and ask. If you feel alone or that you have no support, there are many ways to gather a support group around you. Seek professional support. There are numerous support groups out there and a lot of great counselors. Find a church that you can connect with or even an online forum where people are supporting one another. Don't fight this alone.

APPLICATION: Have an honest discussion with your loved ones about what specifically they can do to help you. Write out statements for them to say to you in times of distress. Let them know what not to say. Help them understand how to best help you.

You Are *Not* Going Crazy

$\mathcal{S}$

Crazy people don't sit around all day wondering if they're nuts.
—DAVID AUBURN, *PROOF*

Let this chapter bring encouragement that *you are not going crazy*. This fear can be real and intense for those struggling with an anxiety disorder. You may never have felt so out of control in your life, and your thoughts are bizarre and irrational—some even violent, sexual, and disturbing. You think, *I have never had thoughts like this before! What is happening?* But the truth is, you have had thoughts like that before, but you never paid much attention to them. You recognized a thought as warped, not in line with your moral values, and you discarded it quickly. Now, these thoughts come at you hourly, and they won't go away! Are you losing your mind? Is this how a psychopath begins their journey? How much longer can you hold it together before you snap and end up as front-page news? You saw the look on your spouse's face when you told them you feared touching doorknobs because of germs. You think that if you confess to your doctor that you have to repeat the Lord's Prayer four times in a row to feel at ease driving over a bridge, he will commit you. I hear you, but you're still not going crazy!

Sixty percent of my anxiety was the fear of my losing control and going completely insane. I would have times when my mind would just shut off and I wouldn't know where I was or what I was supposed to be doing. Some days I was under such severe torment that I couldn't remember my name. I often pictured myself on the front page of the newspaper. "Mother of Five Loses Her Mind and _____" (you fill in the blank). Any way a mother of five could lose her mind, I feared that would happen to me. I had overwhelming thoughts of harm all the time, even intense urges and violent sensations. It was alarming, because I was seriously the type of person—and still am—who feels remorse for stepping on an ant!

There were moments when I was minutes away from checking myself into the mental hospital, thinking that I was a danger to myself or to others. I imagined what my children's lives would be like with their mother in a mental hospital. I thought, without a doubt, that this was how *crazy* started. The thought of how real and traumatic that fear was for me still brings me to tears. It seems irrational to me now in my healthy state, but it was very real in those anxious moments.

The fear of going crazy is very common for those who have an anxiety disorder. I am sure your doctor has told you many times that you are not going crazy. I am sure that your friends and your spouse have, too. But deep down inside you are not sure you can believe them, because your anxious thoughts tell you otherwise. That is why I have devoted an entire chapter to tell you, *"You are not going crazy!"*

Crazy People Don't Know They Are Crazy— They Think They Are Awesome!

The very fact that you are afraid of going crazy shows you how very sane you are. Your mind is overwhelmed. Have you ever tried to rationalize with an overtired toddler? It is impossible! Their fears, rages, and irrational behaviors are clear signs that they are exhausted. Does it mean they are insane? Of course not. It means they need less sugar from Grandma, an earlier bedtime, and some hugs. Hey! Isn't a lot of that what you need, too?

This fear will ease over time as you work through your anxiety. The fear of going crazy was one of the last fears to leave me, because even when the anxiety was much less severe, I feared it coming back. I had to turn that fear completely over to God and trust that when He came to set me free, He would not let me go back. Feel reassured that there is absolutely no evidence to support that those struggling with anxiety are more inclined to snap. You have a deep moral code within you that is stronger than you think, and it has more control over your behavior than you think. All that said, if you are having intense thoughts of suicide or harming yourself or others, please seek medical attention immediately.

God Created Us with Sound Minds

"For God has not given us a spirit of fear, but of power and of love and of a sound mind" (2 Timothy 1:7 NKJV). Anxieties can create odd sensations. Our thoughts can sometimes be too difficult to explain. We can feel disconnected, out of body; we can feel foggy in our minds, or have lapses in memory. We can feel rage one minute and sorrow the next. I'm here to comfort you—this is normal. You are not going crazy. You are overwhelmed, like the toddler we just tried to put to bed. God has created in you a wonderful mind, creative, quick to respond, compassionate, emotional, contemplative, and logical. Your mind is a gift, and its default setting is sound, because God says it is. Trust in the Lord that He is renewing your mind, restoring your soul, and strengthening your body. He has given you a spirit of power, love, and a sound mind. This chaos ravaging your brain will settle as you work through healing your anxiety.

Having to trust God with my own sanity was one of the hardest acts of faith I have ever faced. I was terrified to have to trust God with my mental health. I had no control, or at least that's what it felt like. God kept prompting me, *Can you trust Me for your life, your salvation, your future, even if your mind fails?* That was a very hard question for me to answer, and it caused a lot of wrestling. However, in some storms in life you get to a point where there is nothing you can do but trust God. And really, what choice do you have?

∾

APPLICATION: Treat this fear of going crazy in the same way as you do in taking your thoughts captive. If this fear is extremely distressing, seek professional help in working through the fear. Don't self-diagnose on the Internet.

Day 17

Extensions of Anxiety

❧

One small crack does not mean you are broke; it means that you were put to the test and you didn't fall apart.

—LINDA POINDEXTER

I am sure, after battling anxiety, that you are aware how bizarre this disorder can be. I experienced almost every extension of anxiety you can imagine, from the physical sensations to the fear of going crazy all the way to depression and OCD. Today we're going to dip our toes into the water just a bit, to further understand this disorder.

My OCD Story

I sat in my doctor's office trying to convince him that I wasn't *that* bad. My husband held my hand as my doctor calmly encouraged me that I really needed help. He was right, I really did.

Everything was overwhelming to me. I was overstimulated by sounds and lights, and my body shook uncontrollably. My anxiety was beyond control at this point, and I knew something wasn't right as I soon found myself taking on a whole different side of fear I never knew existed: harm OCD. It started with trying to hide my medications from myself so I wouldn't overdose on them. I put bottles of bleach up high and refused to use them with the laundry in case I might drink them. I would buckle in panic if I saw a belt or a rope lying around, thinking I might strangle myself with it. I cried preparing meals, because I hated using knives. I shook opening a bottle of Tylenol, because what if I lost my mind and took the whole thing? I clenched my fists as I drove the car into the garage, because what if I left it on and stayed in it?

I was petrified of anything that I could do or use to harm myself. I will never forget the look on my husband's face when I shared with him the thoughts I was wrestling with. Was I going crazy? Was I suicidal? We didn't know. All I knew was that my fears were tormenting me and my common sense had no say in the matter. Fear of suicide gripped me. (I didn't realize how much our culture talks about this or even jokes about this until I became afraid of it.) Every day, hours upon hours per day, repetitive harm thoughts flooded my mind. I was 100 percent consumed. I would have coffee with a friend, and as they talked, all I could focus on, obsessively, was the scarf around my friend's neck. What if? What if I strangled myself with it?

Most of us know OCD, obsessive-compulsive disorder, as habitual impulses some people have. We usually associate it with a need for absolute cleanliness or excessive hand washing. What I didn't realize was that OCD behaviors begin with anxious thoughts. The *compulsions* are formed to ease the intensity of the fearful thoughts the person is having. If washing your hands five times wasn't enough to shake the thought that you could be contaminated with Ebola, after trial and error,

washing seven times eased the anxiety, and a formula was created. Washing hands seven times means I won't die. That is
the more familiar form of OCD. Harm OCD is actually a more
common form that people battle. It is an extreme fear of hurting yourself or others brought on by violent, repetitive, disturbing, unwanted thoughts. Sounds awful, doesn't it?

The average brain thinks a million thoughts a day, and many
of them are inappropriate, bizarre, and harmful. How does the
average person respond to these thoughts? We laugh them off.
We say to ourselves, *That was dumb!* Or we simply ignore them
and carry on. A person suffering from OCD grabs that thought
and analyzes the validity of it, over and over and over again,
hence the term "obsessive."

I was fortunate that I was able to step out of this before I
started any debilitating ritualistic behaviors to ease the thoughts,
though I was very close. Hiding medications and saying repetitive prayers were signs that I was headed there. My doctor kept
a close eye on me with this, constantly asking me if I was doing
any ritualistic behaviors to ease the intensity of the thoughts.
People who begin "compulsions" know what they are doing is
odd, and they don't want to do the rituals. But the what-ifs are
too powerful to risk giving them up.

Please do not go through this alone. Get help. Doctors and
therapists are well equipped to handle your thoughts. I know
from firsthand experience how hard it is to talk to someone.
The looks on people's faces when I was brave enough to share
what was happening in my mind were often full of confusion, concern, or fear. However, as secret as this condition is
for many people, it is commonly understood by doctors and

mental health professionals. My doctor never batted an eye. He said calmly and firmly, as I trembled in his office waiting for him to *admit* me, "You are not suicidal; you are not going to hurt yourself." My therapist had the same response. (I thought they were lying and signing admission papers behind my back.)

I feel the Lord supernaturally delivered me from OCD. I remember the day I was obsessing over a rope I saw lying on the bathroom floor. (I have five kids. They love taking ropes and belts and tying them on things, so they get left around the house all the time!) I was beyond anxious at the thought and so weary of this mental battle. I attended my weekly Bible study that night a complete wreck. I was doing a lot better anxiety-wise, and I was getting a bit embarrassed about always being the one needing prayer. However, I was desperate, and I cried out before God. In that moment, as I was receiving prayer, I felt a complete peace come over me, and I felt strongly that God had a purpose in all of this brokenness.

Depression

"Anxiety in the heart of man causes depression, but a good word makes it glad" (Proverbs 12:25 NKJV). Can you imagine being tormented day after day after day? How does that not turn into depression? They go hand in hand. Please do not let your depression get too far; seek help.

Depression is something I have battled on and off since my midthirties. I had never struggled with depression when I was younger, even through all the hard years of being a single mom.

This is the difference between clinical depression (a diagnosis) and situational depression (my life is horrible right now). However, I can see, looking back, that the thoughts and lies I allowed in were building a foundation for depression later on in my life. That is why taking our thoughts captive as an act of warfare—but also as a preventive measure—is so important in keeping depression away.

Depression is very much a body, mind, and spirit problem. If you are relying solely on your medication for recovery, you may be missing out on the proven additional benefits of daily exercise and community involvement. It can also be unwise to refuse counseling or medical help and focus only on the spiritual healing of severe depression. Know that as you work on your body, mind, and spirit, you will be helping your depression, too.

Feeling depressed from time to time is common; it can simply be a sign of fatigue, or the weariness of going through a personal crisis, but feeling depressed all the time is not healthy and must be treated. Signs to look out for are exhaustion, emotional numbness or emotional ups and downs, crying all the time, a lack of interest in doing what you love, or a lack of drive and ambition. There are a lot of physical symptoms, too. Talk to your doctor if you think you are suffering from depression.

Despair

I will never forget the day God broke through my depression. I was folding laundry, feeling completely numb and in total despair. I began to sob uncontrollably and begged God to lift it. Like a television show interrupted by a breaking news story, an image of me at one of my children's future weddings flashed into my mind, and my soul leaped. Soon I saw an image of me holding grandchildren and holding my husband's hand at my children's graduations, and baptisms, and more. I soaked it all in, and I began to sob, thanking God for lifting my soul. What I was receiving was a download of hope and promise from the Lord.

I was gifted with hope that there was goodness ahead, that I was just in a season, and I would soon be out. Hope that I didn't have to wait until heaven for life to be good, but that I *would* actually witness and be part of joy, pleasure, blessing, and more in this lifetime, while I am still here. This supernatural download of hope lifted me up enough to see over the waters. I never hit a low like that again. Anytime I would feel that depression or hopelessness creep in, I would say out loud, "I *will* see the goodness of the Lord in the land of the living." Sometimes over and over and over again.

David frequently talks about the state of his soul in the Psalms: "To You, O Lord, I lift up my soul. O my God, I trust in You" (25:1–2 NKJV). He relied on God to protect his soul, because he knew he was inclined to despair, hopelessness, and depression. His circumstances overwhelmed him as he hid from his enemies, afraid to sleep, afraid to come out. However, David was able to hang on to hope, because he declared God the keeper of his soul and asked for a supernatural download of hope for his future. "You will show me the path of life; in Your presence is fullness of joy; at Your right hand are pleasures forevermore" (Psalm 16:11 NKJV).

❧

APPLICATION: When you feel depressing or obsessive thoughts coming on, stop, acknowledge the thoughts, and then think of something positive, for example, a memory or a funny movie you love. Seek medical and professional help for the other struggles related to anxiety. OCD and depression should not be left untreated.

Day 18

Love Casts Out Fear

❧

There is no fear in love. But perfect love drives out fear, because fear has to do with punishment. The one who fears is not made perfect in love.

—1 JOHN 4:18 NIV

Do you constantly correct your behaviors? Do you feel guilty all the time over things that are not that bad? Do you avoid God in shame, feeling that you have to get yourself together first before you can ask anything of Him? Do you feel some days that you are a burden to others and to God? These are all questions we consider when we are not 100 percent convinced of God's undying love for us.

I knew theoretically that God loved me, but it wasn't until I hit rock bottom that His love became a complete reality and healing force in my walk out of anxiety. I discovered it through the encouragement and prayers of others, but the main source of discovering God's love was in the Word. In my season of mental anguish, I was supernaturally given the grace and the motivation to read through the entire Bible front to back. I praise God for the bed rest that allowed me to set time aside for His Word. I told myself that if my mind was failing and my body was weak, I could at least strengthen my spirit. So for weeks and months I rested in bed and read the Word of God, journaling every step of the way. I was looking for hard evidence that He indeed loved me, because everyone kept telling me that love casts out fear.

Reading the Bible in part is good—an important habit to get into. But reading the Word as a whole, from beginning to end, can be life changing. I have to be honest and tell you that I was very hesitant. My mind was vulnerable, and everything set me off. I was worried that when I read through the entire Bible I would be judged, condemned, and rebuked by it. I was scared that it would confirm my belief that I was this ill because God was punishing me. I was also afraid it would reveal how pathetic my faith really was.

Instead, I read a story of a God who loves us furiously, a God who will do anything to keep us from perishing. I read of a God so humble and gentle that He touched the face of a leper in front of a culture who scorned him. I learned about a God so compassionate that He ministered to prostitutes, tax collectors, untouchables, and the most rejected. I read story after story of God's forgiveness and how many times He exerted His power and strength to turn His people back to Him, just so He could call them sons and daughters. Through reading the entire story of God, I found His love.

What happened as I read was what I have been speaking to you about this whole time. I had many negative thoughts about God, many lies and false beliefs that I needed deliverance from. As I read the Bible every day, His truth—the Word—renewed my mind! It began to take captive my lies and hold up the truth against them. It tore down arguments that claimed that God was against me, not for me. It broke the power of the ideas that Satan had me trapped forever and that healing was impossible. After studying His Word, my mind became convinced that God loved me. As I read, my mind began to be renewed, and I realized that truly there was nothing I could do or fear that could separate me from our loving Father. However, even with all this mind renewal, the truth had not quite hit my heart.

Then I had a dream. I was standing in the basement of a house. It was a house I had never been in before. I entered the upper room of the house to explore it further. It was a nice house—full of everything one would need for comfort and security. And in the house stood a man. The man turned to me and said, *I am the Son, welcome to* our *Father's house.*

Oh! That's where we are, my Father's house! I thought (because in my dream I had never actually met my Father before). The Son showed me around the home and could not stop talking about how amazing *our* Father was. He knew Him well, and I was a bit embarrassed that I didn't know Him at all. Then the door began to open, and everyone in the room stood at attention as if royalty were arriving. The man said excitedly, *Father's home!*

In walked the Father. The Father walked toward the Son, and I took it all in. When the Father held His Son's face in His hands, the look of love, pride, and adoration for His Son was jaw-dropping. I had never witnessed such a powerful exchange of love in my life. No Hollywood movie ever came close. I was in awe, mesmerized by it, and then I was saddened. I stood at attention, afraid to be noticed or do something wrong. What was the protocol for Father coming home? I didn't know. My thoughts were very clear: Wow, *there is no way* our *Father will ever love me as much as He loves His Son.* My head hung in shame as I mulled over all of my weaknesses and sins, and my hands fidgeted behind my back. I was ashamed to be there. I just wanted to run and hide.

But before my thought was complete, the Father came and stood before me, like an officer inspecting his troops. I tensed, and He lifted my face and looked at me. He intensely looked at me. His eyes were filled with the most intense adoration, the most furious love I had ever felt. I still have a hard time articulating it, and my eyes are too blurry with tears to see the keys as I type this revelation. His love for me in this dream was as intense and real as it was for His Son. In this dream I never knew my Father, but He knew me, and He loved me passionately. Not one ounce of His being was disappointed in me or disapproving.

I awoke from this dream completely changed. No one witnesses the love of God face-to-face without being transformed completely. I knew this dream came as a direct message from heaven. He loves me—deeply and patiently—and there is *nothing* I can do or say or be that will ever change that. It was this revelation that broke the final grip fear had over me.

Why Does Love *Cast Out* Fear?

Fear is a disillusionment, telling us that God is not who He says He is. That is a lie, and fear is powerless. Love is a real depiction of the nature of God. It is tangible and it is powerful. When we truly grasp God's love for us, then we link eyes with our Father, and we begin to understand the security we have in His love. It becomes our strong foundation. Saul, having tried religion and having been zealous for the law, had an encounter with the love of God. He was a murderer; he persecuted God's church and killed His saints. After all the evil things Saul/Paul did in the eyes of God, he came to one conclusion following his encounter with the truth of Jesus Christ. He wrote, "And I pray that you, being rooted and established in love, may have power, together with all the Lord's holy people, to grasp how wide and long and high and deep is the love of Christ, and to know this love that surpasses knowledge—that you may be filled to the measure of all the fullness of God" (Ephesians 3:17–19 NIV).

Many people have tried to explain the love of God. They have written books and taught sermons; but all the messages, all the songs, all the stories will never account for the reality of His love. Paul said it would take prayer to even grasp how wide and long and high and deep is the love of Christ. What does it mean to *grasp*? It means to seize hold of, to hold on to with all of your strength, to hold firmly.

When I was able to grasp even a small glimpse with all my heart and mind of the love of God, I was able to open up to receive it. I could allow myself to imagine Him saying, *I am very proud of you.* Or *Way to go, you did that well.* Or *I love you, Sarah.* Or *Don't be afraid; I have good things in store for you.* I'd never had self-thoughts like that before; I was an extremely shamed-filled person. This was a foreign voice. As soon as I opened up that space in my heart and mind, God's thoughts flooded in and cleared out the torment.

This knowledge of God's love is something the enemy will try to rob us of, all the time. Through our sins, shame, guilt, and condemnation, Satan will try to convince us we are unworthy of God's love. He is right, to a degree; we are undeserving. That is what makes His love amazing and beyond human comparison. God does not love us the same way we experience or give love. Love is who He is. It has power. Love is unbreakable and unmoving, no matter how horrible you think you are.

God wanted one thing from you when He created you. He asked that you love Him in return with all of your heart, your mind, and your soul. This is your life's purpose, the only thing you are striving to accomplish. Will He love you any less if you don't? No! However, when you seek His love and find it, you are set free!

❧

APPLICATION: Challenge yourself to read through the Bible with the sole intent of seeking God's love. When you read through the Scriptures, ask God to reveal His love through His Word. Mark that revelation in your Bible.

Day 19

Get Up and Go!

❧

"Go back?" he thought. "No good at all! Go sideways? Impossible! Go forward? Only thing to do! On we go!" So up he got, and trotted along with his little sword held in front of him and one hand feeling the wall, and his heart all of a patter and a pitter.
—J. R. R. TOLKIEN, *THE HOBBIT*

I will never fully understand the ways of God. He blesses us when we least deserve it. He gives us great tasks when we feel unqualified, and He sometimes tells us to move on when we are not ready to. Living with crippling anxiety is all-consuming and draining. I understand completely how debilitating anxiety and depression can be. You're terrified; you don't know which way is up. And I am in total agreement with you that this is an extremely difficult season. However, as this book is coming to a close, it might be time for you to push forward. I want to share with you a mini Bible study about moving forward.

God's chosen people, the Israelites, were in bondage. Through generations of turning their backs on God, they found themselves enslaved in Egypt. Their bondage was so severe and so intolerable that they cried out to God for freedom. Then God chose a man, Moses, as the one who would deliver His people. "And the LORD said: 'I have surely seen the oppression of My people who are in Egypt, and have heard their cry because of their taskmasters, for I know their sorrows. So I have come down to deliver them out of the hand of the Egyptians, and to bring them up from that land to a good and large land, to a land flowing with milk and honey'" (Exodus 3:7–8 NKJV).

God had one objective in mind: *Set My people free!* Moses reluctantly headed to Egypt to tell the people of God's plan to rescue them. Pharaoh was stubborn, Moses was discouraged, and the Israelites thought it was crazy. Moses prayed in desperation to God, thinking that the call was too much and near impossible. Then God said to Moses:

Therefore say to the children of Israel: "I am the LORD; I will bring you out from under the burdens of the Egyptians, *I will rescue you from their bondage*, and I will redeem you with an outstretched arm and with great judgments. I will take you as My people, and I will be your God. Then you shall know that I am the LORD your God who brings you out from under the burdens of the Egyptians. And I will bring you into the land which I swore to give to Abraham, Isaac, and Jacob; and I will give it to you as a heritage: I am the LORD." So Moses spoke thus to the children of Israel; *but they did not heed Moses, because of anguish of spirit and cruel bondage.*

EXODUS 6:6–9 NKJV (EMPHASIS MINE)

Do you have a hard time believing that God will set you free? Maybe you have read through the last eighteen days of this book saying to yourself, *This is good, but it won't work for me.*

I have already tried. Sometimes when we have been in bondage for a long time, our spirits are crushed, and we lose the fight. We accept our bondage; we identify ourselves with it. We say to ourselves and to others, "This is just the way I am. Deal with it!"

You make plans daily, monthly, and yearly around *your* anxiety. It makes the decisions for you. You stopped trying to be free, and your family and friends have learned to tiptoe around *your anxiety* and to accommodate it. It has now become who you are. I have been in that frame of mind. If I'd had a T-shirt that read "I have anxiety," I would have worn it day and night. I made plans for how I was going to cope and live with this cruel bondage forever. What would it look like at forty, at fifty, at eighty? Would I be the anxious grandmother doped up on Ativan? Would my grandchildren know not to stress me out too much? I began accepting my anxiety as my fate, as my future, and as my identity. "Therefore say to the children of Israel: '...I will rescue you from [your] bondage'...But they did not heed Moses, because of anguish of spirit and cruel bondage."

When you have been in captivity for a long time, you can forget what freedom looks like. Maybe you have been this way even since childhood. Perhaps you have skimmed over the parts where I promise you freedom, thinking, *Yeah, yeah, I've heard it before.* If you see yourself in this, you need to stop and listen. God has His hand outstretched to you, and He wants to deliver you from this oppression. Choosing your anxiety as your identity is a submission to bondage, a refusal to leave Egypt, and a rejection of God's salvation power.

God used His power through Moses. And finally, after plagues, including locusts, frogs, hail, and the death of the first-born sons, Pharaoh let Moses take his slaves. The people who had been resisting their freedom had no choice at that point. God had cleared the way for them to be free. They had to go with Moses because their whole life of slavery had just been destroyed. God made it very clear that *He* was not leaving without them.

Do you feel God tugging on you to face some of your issues, and you're terrified? Do you tend to shove down the reality of how entangled in bondage you are? Is God pushing you to a place you don't want to be? We all like to skip to the bit about the parting of the waters in the Exodus story, but we need to slow down. The Israelites had some other problems to work out first. What I am about to show you deeply impacted me and my walk out of mental slavery.

Pharaoh, deep in mourning and too distraught to chase after the Israelites, buried his head in grief, and the great *exodus* began. Twice in Exodus 13, Moses reminded the children of God that God had indeed just released them from the "house of bondage" (vv. 3, 14 NKJV). You would think they would rejoice; you would think they would be thankful. But they didn't feel very free. They had nothing; they didn't know where they were going or what was happening next. They were angered that God had turned their lives upside down. But God continued to lead them forward. "Then it came to pass, when Pharaoh had let the people go, that God did not lead them by way of the land of the Philistines, *although that was near*; for God said, *'Lest perhaps the people change their minds when they see war, and return to*

Egypt.' So God led the people around by way of the wilderness of the Red Sea" (Exodus 13:17–18 NKJV; emphasis mine).

What? God had a plan to set them free and led them the *long* way out?! He could have walked them straight out and into the Promised Land in days! What was going on? Do you ever get angry that God hasn't just lifted this off? Or miraculously taken you out of this prison of fear? Why is God taking so long? The answer is simple: He never, ever wants you to return to this bondage again—ever.

God said to Moses: *If I give them the easy way out, the minute life gets tough again they will run right back to Egypt.* If you don't do the hard work—exercising, praying, going to therapy, and taking your thoughts captive—the minute life throws you a curveball, or puts a heavy weight of pressure on you, you will be right back here. I know you don't want that. I know that you have said to yourself, *I never, ever, ever want to go through this again!* If you are obedient to follow God and follow Him the hard way out, you will never have to. Moses led the Israelites toward the Red Sea, and God, whose desire is to set His people free forever, did a very odd thing. He made things worse!

Now the LORD spoke to Moses, saying: "Speak to the children of Israel, that they turn and camp before Pi Hahiroth, between Migdol and the sea, opposite Baal Zephon; you shall camp before it by the sea. For Pharaoh will say of the children of Israel, 'They are bewildered by the land; the wilderness has closed them in.' Then *I will harden Pharaoh's heart,* so that he will pursue them; and I will gain honor over Pharaoh and over all his army, that the Egyptians may know that I am the LORD." And they did so.

Now it was told the king of Egypt that the people had fled, and the heart of Pharaoh and his servants was turned against the people; and they said, "Why have we done this, that we have let Israel go from serving us?" So he made ready his chariot and took his people with him. Also, he took six hundred choice chariots, and *all the chariots of Egypt* with captains over every one of them. *And the LORD hardened the heart of Pharaoh king of Egypt, and he pursued the children of Israel*; and the children of Israel went out with boldness. So the Egyptians pursued them, all the horses and chariots of Pharaoh, his horsemen and his army, and overtook them camping by the sea beside Pi Hahiroth, before Baal Zephon.

EXODUS 14:1–9 NKJV (EMPHASIS MINE)

God led the Israelites into an overwhelming wilderness and then hardened Pharaoh's heart. Pharaoh was so enraged that he pursued them with *all* of his army. Do you feel that in this journey of mental breakdown everything has come up against you? Your marriage, your past pains, your weaknesses, your sins? Do you feel closed in? Unable to move, or even know where to begin? Do you know that this is perhaps God's plan? Or do you think it's all a cruel joke?

The Israelites were stuck—in over their heads. *Apparently* God was leading them out of bondage, but they felt more entrapped and out of control than they ever had before in their lives. They even forgot that they had been the ones requesting freedom to begin with! They hadn't expected it to be this scary and life threatening. Soon the Israelites, exhausted and terrified, saw *the entire army* of Pharaoh charging toward them! Can you imagine? How would you have reacted?

> And when Pharaoh drew near, the children of Israel lifted their eyes, and behold, the Egyptians marched after them. So *they were very afraid*, and the children of Israel cried out to the LORD. Then they said to Moses, "Because there were no graves in Egypt, have you taken us away to die in the wilderness? Why have you so dealt with us, to bring us up out of Egypt? Is this not the word that we told you in Egypt, saying, 'Let us alone that we may serve the Egyptians'? For it would have been better for us to serve the Egyptians than that we should die in the wilderness."
>
> EXODUS 14:10–12 NKJV (EMPHASIS MINE)

What the heck, Moses?! Did you bring us out here to die?!

You tried to be set free, and it's only getting worse. You think, *God! What is going on? Have You brought me all the way out here to kill me?!* I had this feeling many times, and I made sure I articulated to God how angry I was at Him for letting this happen to me. I would pray for deliverance, and things just seemed to get worse. I didn't understand why God—who promised to deliver me—would do this. Not only were the Israelites angry and terrified, but they begged Moses to return them to their bondage! They were coping well in their captivity; this freedom thing was too risky. Well, my beloved, God doesn't want you to just *cope*! He wants you free!

Moses had compassion on them, probably because they were distraught and probably because he doubted this exodus himself. So Moses comforted the people and then knelt before God, whose response is surprising: "And Moses said to the people, 'Do not be afraid. Stand still, and see the salvation of the LORD, which He will accomplish for you today. For the Egyptians whom you see today, you shall see again no more forever. The LORD will fight for you, and you shall hold your peace.' And the LORD said to Moses, 'Why do you cry to Me? *Tell the children of Israel to go forward*'" (Exodus 14:13–15 NKJV; emphasis mine).

Did God seriously just tell Moses to shut up and move on? Yes, He did. Is it time? Is it time for you to stop petitioning God and start moving forward? Let's finish with God leading Moses and the children to the Red Sea; don't skip a thing.

> Then Moses stretched out his hand over the sea; and the LORD caused the sea to go back by a strong east wind all that night, and made the sea into dry land, and the waters were divided. So the children of Israel went into the midst of the sea on the dry ground, and the waters were a wall to them on their right hand and on their left. And *the Egyptians pursued* and went after them into the midst of the sea, *all* Pharaoh's horses, his chariots, and his horsemen.
>
> Now it came to pass, in the morning watch, that the LORD looked down upon the army of the Egyptians through the pillar of fire and cloud, and He troubled the army of the Egyptians. And He took off their chariot wheels, so that they drove them with difficulty; and the

Egyptians said, "Let us flee from the face of Israel, for the LORD fights for them against the Egyptians."

Then the LORD said to Moses, "Stretch out your hand over the sea, that the waters may come back upon the Egyptians, on their chariots, and on their horsemen." And Moses stretched out his hand over the sea; and when the morning appeared, the sea returned to its full depth, while the Egyptians were fleeing into it. So *the LORD over-threw the Egyptians in the midst of the sea.* Then the waters returned and covered the chariots, the horsemen, *and all the army of Pharaoh that came into the sea* after them. *Not so much as one of them remained.* But the children of Israel had walked on dry land in the midst of the sea, and the waters were a wall to them on their right hand and on their left.

So the LORD saved Israel that day out of the hand of the Egyptians, and Israel saw the Egyptians dead on the seashore. *Thus Israel saw the great work which the LORD had done in Egypt; so the people feared the LORD, and believed the LORD and His servant Moses.*

EXODUS 14:21–31 NKJV (EMPHASIS MINE)

God allowed His people to go through great suffering and hard work. He allowed for everything to come against them at once. Why? Because He defeated it all at once! When it is all coming at you, and it's all just too much, know that God is going to deal with it *all*! If you struggle with an addiction and you don't deal with the heart and the habits, then you will surely run right back into bondage. If you don't deal with the root causes, your spiritual starvation, your unwavering thoughts, you will return to your bondage of fear, time and time again. Trust that God is doing a great work in you.

Know that there is a time to rest and receive reassurance and help—and then there is a time for you to get up and move forward. And it won't be when you *feel* like it! It will be when God says so. Months into my breakdown I planned a trip across the continent with my two best friends, assuming I would be better by then. It was to be the girls' trip of a lifetime. It was weeks away, and I was far from better—I was worse! I hadn't even been able to grocery shop for my family yet. How the heck was I going to hop on a plane and travel away from my family, my bed, and my security? I prepared myself to call my friends and cancel. I would just eat the cost of the plane ticket. So I prayed and asked God if I should go. (By the way, I was terrified of flying!)

The Lord said to me, *Go! It will be good for you.* Go?! I can't even leave my house for twenty minutes without racing back to my bed. I can't eat at restaurants; I can't be around a lot of people! *Sarah, it's time get up and move forward,* the Lord kept nudging.

I went. It was hard and terrifying, and at times embarrassing. I felt guilty that I was ruining my friends' trip with my neediness, but they were supportive and patient. It turned out to be the best thing for me, and I came back freer. That push created momentum in me. It reinstilled confidence that I could keep going. I could get on with my life and know that wherever I was in the world, God was still with me. Slowly, from that time on, I got stronger and stronger and stronger. If it hadn't been for God throwing me into the deep end with that trip, I think I might still be in bondage to my fears.

I rejoice often that I am free; I don't ever want to go back. God propelled me to deliverance against my will some days, while I kicked and fought Him the whole way, but He had one objective in mind: my freedom. He has one objective in mind for you, too: your deliverance. It's time now to get up and move forward!

APPLICATION: What is one thing you can do right away that you have been avoiding? What is one risk you can take to push yourself back into life? Make a decision to take a step forward every day. Expect good days and bad, and rejoice in the victories!

Day 20

Staying Free

In almost everything that touches our everyday life on earth, God is pleased when we're pleased. He wills that we be as free as birds to soar and sing our maker's praise without anxiety.

—A. W. TOZER, "HOW THE LORD LEADS"

Living free from anxiety is extremely possible! I'm a living testament, and I have met many others who are as well. My therapist was convinced I would get through this. He also said that when I did, I would be better for it. I thought *he* was the crazy one. It turned out he was right. You would be surprised to know how many people have gone through a season like this in their lifetimes and have come out stronger on the other end. I never thought I would be able to run again, as I have been recently. I thought this anxiety would certainly cripple me for life. However, I am running, but I run strategically now—with the Lord's strength, not my own. My strength has been renewed and so will yours.

Even the youths shall faint and be weary,
And the young men shall utterly fall,
But those who wait on the LORD

Shall renew their strength;
They shall mount up with wings like eagles,
They shall run and not be weary,
They shall walk and not faint.

Isaiah 40:30–31 NKJV

Take a moment now to see how far you have come. Even the smallest victories are worth celebrating. At this point in recovery you will have to maintain a healthy body, mind, and spirit. This balance must be set for the rest of your life. Do not be discouraged. It will be worth it. Freedom is something that will have to be maintained. It is one thing to beat an anxiety disorder; it is another thing to stay free from it. I want to show you some ways to stay free from crippling fear.

Know your emotions. You will feel anxious again; I can promise you that, because anxiety is a human emotion. I know you understand the difference between irrational fear and natural anxiety over a situation. I remember feeling excited to have butterflies in my stomach in one situation. "Regular old nerves!" I celebrated. I was thrilled to be reacting naturally and not in terror. As I was being set free from anxiety and was healing, I was a bit uptight and afraid to *feel* any emotion, because I didn't want to go back there—ever. I had been traumatized by the whole experience. However, learning that emotions are good, and that it is healthy for me to acknowledge them, took time and trust. We don't have to fear our emotions, but we can't let them dominate our lives, either. Always remember that you're the boss over your feelings and thoughts. They don't and shouldn't control you.

Take care of your body. Taking care of your body's health is a deal you're not allowed to break. This will have to be a steady habit built into your life, like brushing your teeth or checking Facebook. Physical exercise, proper nutrition, and rest will ensure stability throughout your entire physiological state, not to mention that you'll live longer!

Learn better stress management. I had someone ask me if I could handle as much stress now as I did before my breakdown, and I answered, "No, I can't handle as much stress as I did before, but I never should have been able to handle that much to begin with." I realized that it's not that I can handle less stress now, it is that I can handle only what is healthy for me. Before my breakdown, I pushed myself past the point of what was good for me, and I called it being "strong." I just can't do that anymore. I now know to handle stress before it handles me. Know the signs that you are getting overwhelmed and stressed. Is your breathing tense? Are you not sleeping? Are you eating too much or too little? You know yourself. What signs do you give when you are stressed? Watch out for those, and do not let things get out of control. Keep rest a priority and do not forget time with the Lord.

Build boundaries. Think of your life as a garden, with plants and flowers and beautifully organized arrangements of shrubbery. Think about how much work it takes to maintain it. Think about who or what gets to enter and who or what will walk all over you and destroy your garden. Set boundaries for your life and for yourself. Don't let people or situations drain you or use you. Learn to speak up, ask for what you need, and for goodness' sake, *say no!* Don't let guilt and passivity leave tread marks on your sanity. Guard yourself well.

Stay connected. Find your community. Work on building friendships and family relationships. Relationships and community are essential to mental health. We actually moved to a small town in search of community for our family. The blessing it has been to be a part of a community has been enormous—reviving! Invest in your relationships and watch the blessings come back to you.

Do what you love. Always do what you love. Find your passion, find your gifting, explore what God has for you, live and enjoy life! *Laugh*, have fun! Spend money, go on trips, eat cake! When God created Adam and Eve, He saw all that He had made and offered it to Adam and Eve for their joy and pleasure. God wants you to enjoy the life He has given you.

Stay close to God. Do not neglect your relationship with God. He is and will always be the sustainer and provider of all our needs and blessings. We need to know Him more. He wants us to share ourselves openly with Him. Reading the Word of God and praying can seem like a chore sometimes, but so does playing a game with our kids when we are tired, or going on a date with our spouse when we are broke. We know that it is essential to make sacrifices of time and money to maintain healthy relationships with those we love. The same goes for our relationship with our heavenly Father.

Cast all your cares on God. Go to God for everything, and I mean everything. If you bump your toe, go to God. If you lose your job, go to God. He cares for it all. Learning to go to God for all of our needs—physical, emotional, spiritual, and mental—will keep us connected to Him in a much deeper way and free us from unchecked stress and fear.

Don't strive. Watch for signs of striving: Are you working extra hours to earn approval from man or from God? Check your motives. This is the one thing that will send you right back into bondage if you let it go too far. It is godly to work hard and run after your plans and goals. However, it is your motives that ensnare you, not the destination. Always evaluate: Why are you taking things on, and for whose glory?

Guard your thoughts. The first place anxiety will try to reenter is your thoughts. You will have to be on guard for the rest of your life, guarding your mind. It won't be as tiresome as it is now. Once you take control, your mind begins to renew and think differently, for good! That's exciting. However, every once in a while those warped thoughts and lies will try to creep back in, but you don't have to worry about it, because you know what to do.

I am very proud of you for coming this far. I can promise you that when you finally get through this anxiety journey, you will be stronger than you were before this all began. You will have built resilience and healthy habits. You will have more control over your thoughts and a closer relationship with God. But most of all, you will be *fearless*!

❧

APPLICATION: What habits will you develop to ensure good mental health? Reflect on what may have contributed to your breakdown in the past (for example, lack of boundaries, bad health habits, lack of sleep). Learn from yourself and make some changes!

Praise

I would maintain that thanks are the highest form of thought,
and that gratitude is happiness doubled by wonder.

—G. K. CHESTERTON, *A SHORT HISTORY OF ENGLAND*

The final day is here. *Wow!* What a day to celebrate and be thankful for! You have made it this far, and I know you will continue to get stronger every day. Two chapters ago, on Day 19, we walked with the Israelites out of the "house of bondage" (Egypt). They were hesitant, stubborn, terrified, and completely overwhelmed. But they did it; or I should say, *God did it!* The seas parted, Pharaoh's entire army was swallowed up, and the Israelites were set free. "Then Moses and the Israelites sang this song...: 'I will sing to the LORD, for he is highly exalted. Both horse and driver he has hurled into the sea. The LORD is my strength and my defense; he has become my salvation. He is my God, and I will praise him, my father's God, and I will exalt him'" (Exodus 15:1–2 NIV).

When you are rescued from an overwhelming circumstance, the praise must be turned back to God, in thankfulness and worship. He saw your captivity, He has exerted his strength to set you free, and He has lifted you out of many waters. He is our first responder, our emergency surgeon, our greatest counselor. He deserves our praise. From this point on, if we continue to bathe our thoughts in praise and thankfulness, we will wash our minds daily of toxic thoughts and feelings. Praise and thankfulness remind us not only of all God has done and will do, but that we are loved and cared for. Praise should be on our tongues quickly in all circumstances and trials.

We have learned the hard way how far we can slip from God when we are not guarding our thoughts. We have to remember that we don't have to be healed completely to begin praising Him. Often we avoid spending time in God's presence because we feel that we have to clean house before He gets here, like cleaning before the housekeeper comes. He wants our messy hearts, our mangled minds, our weaknesses, and our anxieties, too. It is okay to feel broken and thankful at the same time. It is okay to vent before the Lord and praise Him in the same sentence. It is okay to scream into your pillow and then worship Him in the next breath. David did. This is called "praising Him anyway."

When we praise Him anyway, He turns our mourning into dancing and replaces our robes of *despair* with garments of praise. "Provide for those who grieve in Zion—to bestow on them a crown of beauty instead of ashes, the oil of joy instead of mourning, and a garment of praise instead of a spirit of despair. They will be called oaks of righteousness, a planting of the LORD for the display of his splendor" (Isaiah 61:3 NIV).

The very first day of this book, we came to understand fear as misplaced worship. This last day we are going to make a conscious decision to turn our worship back to God. It is time now to avert our eyes from our trials and ourselves and to turn to worship God. He is strengthening us, and it is our thankfulness that will keep us from heading back to bondage and keep us moving forward.

God never stops refining us. He has a completed version of us in mind, and for the rest of our lives we will be molded and shaped to be more like Him. Imagine yourself stronger, more loving, peaceful, happy, and prosperous—that is God's purpose for you. These trials that we dread in life are taking us there. When we have a heart of gratitude for what the Lord is doing in our hearts and in our lives, it changes our perspective, from *Woe is me* to *Holy is He.*

I knew I was receiving healing victory when I had good moments. Then I had good minutes, and then good hours, and, oh, did I praise God and thank Him when I had my very first good day! As you heal, you will have moments when you regress a bit. It is the natural process of recovery in anything, and that's okay. However, rejoice in the good moments, and soon those days will be weeks, months, and then years. Freedom is before you!

God asked one thing of His children when He set them free from slavery: "Be careful that you do not forget the LORD, who brought you out of Egypt, out of the land of slavery" (Deuteronomy 6:12 NIV). Ordinances and celebrations were put in place to help them to be always mindful of where they had come from and how they got out. This will forever be your story; this season must never be forgotten. Always remember what the Lord has done for you. Tell your children, tell your grandchildren, and praise Him for His works! Share your story, help others, and testify to the goodness of God. That is what you do after a grueling season like this.

When we turn our mourning into dancing and our pain into praise, we declare the goodness of God over our lives. When we live in a place of praise, we live in a place of protection. Words can't hurt us, thoughts can't derail us, and fears cannot stand. When we remain hidden in God's love, we are free. That is where complete healing takes place.

I know that you are on a journey out of this bondage. I see lies being broken, hopes being restored, and strength coming back to you. This is the beginning of your journey into total freedom from mental illness. This is the beginning of your own story, from *panic* to *praise*.

❧

APPLICATION: Praise God with all that is in you!

Acknowledgments

"God is going to use this" was the one phrase I heard time and time again from the people in my life. I had a hard time believing them until the moment *Fearless in 21 Days* was placed into my heart. This book would not exist if it weren't for God's family.

I want to start by acknowledging Dr. O. Ukrainetz for guiding me through the storm; your medical, spiritual, and mental guidance saved my life. Thank you to Stephen Kennedy, editor at *Testimony Magazine*, who strongly encouraged me to submit my story "From Panic to Praise"; you launched this story. Thank you to my former church family, Mosaic Christian Fellowship, the little church with the big heart, who loved me through the worst.

A message hidden in darkness is no message at all, which is why I am so grateful for the FaithWords publishing team for their dedication and hard work to see this book released.

I also want to acknowledge Richard Shelston and Carolyn Ouwerkerk for believing in this project and endorsing it during the baby stages. Thank you to Tim Beals, for giving me a big *YES* from the team and welcoming me to the Credo Communications family. Thank you to my literary agent, Karen Neumair. You fueled this project with passion and professionalism; I am so amazed.

Acknowledgments

My greatest gratitude to my lifelong friend, Heather, for your selfless support during your greatest battle; I miss you so much. Thank you to Mom and Dad Ball for your endless support and love. Thank you, Mom, for being the most fearless prayer warrior I have ever known. You prayed this into existence. Thank you, Dad, for sharing your battle stories with me and showing me how to live strongly and resiliently. Finally, to my husband, Kevin, and our five children: Who I am—this book, my heart—they wouldn't exist without you.

Notes

Introduction: Panic to Praise

1. Anxiety Disorders Association of Canada, "Anxiety Disorders," last modified 2007, accessed September 28, 2016, http://www.anxietycanada.ca/english/.

2. Anxiety and Depression Association of America, "Facts & Statistics," last modified August 2016, accessed September 28, 2016, https://adaa.org/about-adaa/press-room/facts-statistics.

Day 1: Creation of Fear

1. R. Reid Wilson, *Don't Panic: Taking Control of Anxiety Attacks* (New York: HarperCollins, 1996), 5–6.

2. Ibid., 140–63.

3. Ibid.

Day 2: Body-Mind Connection

1. Michael W. Otto and Jasper A. J. Smits, *Exercise for Mood and Anxiety: Proven Strategies for Overcoming Depression and Enhancing Well-Being* (New York: Oxford University Press, 2011).

2. Jack Challem. *The Food-Mood Solution* (Hoboken, NJ: Wiley, 2007).

3. Wilson, *Don't Panic*, 290.

Day 3: Stop the Panic

1. Claire Weekes, *Hope and Help for Your Nerves* (New York: Penguin, 1969).

Day 4: Mornings and Evenings

1. B. J. Shannon, R. A. Dosenbach, Y. Su, A. G. Vlassenko, L. J. Larson-Prior, T. S. Nolan, A. Z. Snyder, and M. E. Raichle, "Morning-Evening Variation in Human Brain Metabolism and Memory Circuits," *Journal of Neurophysiology* 109, no. 5 (March 1, 2013): 1444–56, doi:10.1152/jn.00651.2012.

Day 5: Guilt-Free Rest

1. Mark Buchanan, *The Rest of God: Restoring Your Soul by Restoring Sabbath* (Nashville, TN: Thomas Nelson, 2006).

Day 6: Words of Power

1. "Masaru Emoto's Rice Experiment," YouTube video, https://www.youtube.com/watch?v=Ehlw-9PJkIE.

Day 13: Taking Your Thoughts Captive

1. Caroline Leaf, "You Are What You Think: 75–98% of Mental and Physical Illnesses Come from Our Thought Life!" *Dr. Leaf's Blog*, posted November 30, 2011, http://drleaf.com/blog/you-are-what-you-think-75-98-of-mental-and-physical-illnesses-come-from-our-thought-life/.

2. Caroline Leaf, "How to Rewire Your Brain," *Sid Roth's It's Supernatural*, posted February 28, 2011, https://www.youtube.com/watch?v=1xnw9vO8nhM.

Day 14: Spiritual Deliverance

1. Bill Thrasher, *A Journey to Victorious Praying* (Chicago, IL: Moody, 2003).

Bibliography

Anxiety and Depression Association of America. "Facts & Statistics." Last modified August 2016. Accessed September 28, 2016. https://adaa.org/about-adaa/press-room/facts-statistics.

Anxiety Disorders Association of Canada. "Anxiety Disorders." Last modified 2007. Accessed September 28, 2016. http://www.anxietycanada.ca/english/.

Buchanan, Mark. *The Rest of God: Restoring Your Soul by Restoring Sabbath*. Nashville, TN: Thomas Nelson, 2006.

Calm Clinic. "Can Anxiety Be Caused by Dehydration?" http://www.calmclinic.com/anxiety/causes/water-dehydration.

Challem, Jack. *The Food-Mood Solution*. Hoboken, NJ: Wiley, 2007.

Keathley, J. Hampton, III. "Biblical Meditation." Bible.org. https://bible.org/article/biblical-meditation.

Leaf, Caroline. "How to Rewire Your Brain." *Sid Roth's It's Supernatural*. Posted February 28, 2011. https://www.youtube.com/watch?v=1xnw9vO8nhM.

———. "You Are What You Think: 75–98% of Mental and Physical Illnesses Come from Our Thought Life!" *Dr. Leaf's Blog*. Posted November 30, 2011. http://drleaf.com/blog/you-are-what-you-think-75-98-of-mental-and-physical-illnesses-come-from-our-thought-life/.

"Masaru Emoto's Rice Experiment." YouTube video. https://www.youtube.com/watch?v=Ehlw-9PJkIE.

McLean, Peter D. "Mental Health and Mental Illness." Invited Submission to the Standing Senate Committee on Social Affairs, Science and Technology, prepared by the Anxiety Disorders Association of Canada/Association Canadienne des Troubles Anxieux, June 2003. http://anxietycanada.ca/english/pdf/kirby.pdf.

Otto, Michael W., and Jasper A. J. Smits. *Exercise for Mood and Anxiety: Proven Strategies for Overcoming Depression and Enhancing Well-Being.* New York: Oxford University Press, 2011.

Reynolds, Gretchen. "How Exercise Can Calm Anxiety." *New York Times,* July 3, 2013. http://well.blogs.nytimes.com/2013/07/03/how-exercise-can-calm-anxiety/?_r=0.

Shannon, B. J., R. A. Dosenbach, Y. Su, A. G. Vlassenko, L. J. Larson-Prior, T. S. Nolan, A. Z. Snyder, and M. E. Raichle. "Morning-Evening Variation in Human Brain Metabolism and Memory Circuits." *Journal of Neurophysiology* 109, no. 5 (March 1, 2013): 1444–56. doi:10.1152/jn.00651.2012.

Thrasher, Bill. *A Journey to Victorious Praying.* Chicago, IL: Moody, 2003.

Weekes, Claire. *Hope and Help for Your Nerves.* New York: Penguin, 1969.

Wilson, R. Reid. *Don't Panic: Taking Control of Anxiety Attacks.* New York: HarperCollins, 1996.

About the Author

SARAH E. BALL is a blogger, speaker, and mental illness survivor. Her story and fierce truths have brought freedom to many anxiety sufferers. Sarah reaches thousands through her blog saraheball.com, online courses, and powerful speaking. Sarah regularly appears as a host and guest on several national television programs. She is a columnist for *City Light News,* is a regular contributor for FunandFaith.ca, and a regular guest blogger at *To Love, Honor & Vacuum.* Sarah is also the Alberta representative for the Word Guild, Canada's largest Christian Writer's Guild, and works as a faculty member at the annual Write Canada Conference.